TEACHING AND USING BLISSYMBOLICS

Written for use by instructors of communicatively impaired persons.

Eugene T. McDonald, Ed.D.

A publication of the Blissymbolics Communication Institute

ISBN 0-9690516-8-9

Printed in Canada by Garden City Press

80 81 82 83 84   5 4 3 2 1

Index: *Barbara Hehner*
Design: *Jack Steiner Graphic Design*

Ⓑ indicates 1) a symbol which differs from the C. K. Bliss version either in symbol form or accompanying wording or
2) a new BCI symbol authorized in the absence of requested comment from C. K. Bliss.

Many words could be written to express the pleasure of the Blissymbolics Communication Institute in publishing *Teaching and Using Blissymbolics*. Its author, Eugene T. McDonald, brings to it a distinguished academic career in speech pathology and psychology, extensive experience in assessing and teaching cerebral palsied children, and a deep commitment to improving the quality of life of handicapped persons and their families. His direct experience with Blissymbolics is varied: he has established an instructor training centre and a Blissymbolics communication program at the Home of Our Merciful Saviour in Philadelphia; he has delivered many lectures and training presentations on the application of Blissymbols; he has developed an instructor correspondence course which provides Elementary Training to Blissymbolics Communication Institute standards. *Teaching and Using Blissymbolics* is an important contribution to the literature relating to Blissymbolics.

But Blissymbols say it better!

)

1977

BCI ⚓ ♡+! ☺

KELLOGG FOUNDATION ⚓ ⚐+8

ⴧ McD ⇉ \ ☐ › ∑

)(

1980

BCI ♡⁻ ⚓☐ ☐ ‹ ⴧ McD

+ ♡⚓ ⴧ McD

⌄

♡ ♡⌇ + ⚐∅

☉!! ☐ ∑

⊕ ·∨♈ +∑

(

10 ↻ +1980

☐ ‹ ⴧ McD ⊕ | |

» ⚐ ⚐⊕∑ + ⚐☊∩,∑

In the Past

1977

Blissymbolics Communication Institute received wonderful news!
The Kellogg Foundation provided financial assistance.
Dr. Eugene T. McDonald agreed to write a book about Blissymbols.

At the Present Time

1980

BCI proudly publishes this book by Dr. McDonald
and thanks him
for
being sensitive to the needs of non-speaking persons,
focussing his attention upon studying Blissymbols,
realizing the ''power'' of Blissymbols.

In the Future

The 1980's

This book by Dr. McDonald will be used widely
for helping Blissymbol users and Blissymbol instructors.

Shirley McNaughton
Programme Consultant
Blissymbolics Communication Institute
Toronto, 1980

Contents

Preface

Educators, parents, therapists and administrators are becoming increasingly concerned about the large population of children who do not learn to speak intelligibly. There is an active seeking for new ways to help these children communicate. One new way is through the use of Blissymbols.

This book is written as an introduction to Blissymbolics and focuses on how to teach Blissymbols to orally handicapped children. It is written from a practical, rather than a theoretical, point of view. The emphasis is on *how to* use and *how to* teach Blissymbols. The author's objective is to provide the basic information needed to begin teaching a child to use Blissymbols. For that reason documentation has been kept to a minimum. As more people gain experience in teaching Blissymbols, theoretical issues will be identified and investigated and a need for a different type of book will arise. It is the author's hope that this introductory book will lead to a solid grounding in the symbols and system of Blissymbolics which should be a requirement for teachers and researchers.

The author expresses his appreciation for their help in bringing this information together to: Shirley McNaughton and Jinny Storr of the Blissymbolics Communication Institute; Sally Greenberg, Gesselle Garnicki, Kelly Griswald and Wendy Andrea of the Home of the Merciful Saviour for Crippled Children; Patricia Hollingsworth of the Lincoln Intermediate School Unit in Pennsylvania; Anne Warrick of the Ottawa Crippled Children's Treatment Centre; Gwen Mann of the James Robinson School, Markham, Ontario; Barbara J. Reckell of the Marvin Beckman Center in Lansing, Michigan; and Margrit Beesley of the Ontario Crippled Children's Centre, Toronto.

I. Introduction

Why learn about Blissymbolics?

In his thought-provoking short story, "The Country of the Blind," H. G. Wells vividly describes the plight of a sighted person who stumbled into an isolated mountain valley where all the inhabitants were blind and had been so for several generations. Once open to the world, the valley became isolated when a stupendous volcanic eruption closed the mountain passes, trapping several families and cutting them off from the rest of the world. The people developed a self-sufficient agricultural community and, as a genetic condition resulted in a higher incidence of blindness in succeeding generations, they made adjustments in their way of doing things so the blind members could work and play along with the others. Eventually all were blind and there remained no one who could recall what it meant to see. By this time a sophisticated culture had been developed in which blind persons worked productively and lived in harmony.

Into this valley a sighted man stumbled by accident. Upon realizing that the inhabitants were blind, he gloated, recalling the aphorism, "In the country of the blind, the one-eyed man is king." This did not, however, prove to be so. He was such a misfit that he seriously considered allowing a medicine man to remove his eyes so he could marry a blind girl and join the community of the blind, rising from "servitude and inferiority to a level of a blind citizen." Only at the last moment before the surgery did he begin climbing and find his way out of the valley, aware that in the Country of the Blind the two-eyed man had been slave — not king! His inability to experience in the common mode, to think as the others thought, and to share their feelings, made him a misfit — an outcast.

And so it is. A community is a body of people having common organization or common interests. An important feature of a community is *fellowship*, which involves shared experience, activity, interests and feelings. Community membership is frequently denied those who, in some important ways, are different from those who comprise the community. The effect on the excluded individual is devastating. Gregariousness — the tendency to live in groups — is a well-known characteristic of human beings. The need for opportunities to interact socially with others is strong. Infants seem to begin seeking social stimulation when only a few weeks old and, during the first five years, the normally developing child, in the words of Gesell and Ilg, "has steadily penetrated into the cultural milieu." The quantity and quality of one's social interactions have a powerful effect on social-emotional development and influence the child's cognitive functioning.

The importance of communication in enabling one to penetrate the cultural milieu and attain community membership cannot be exaggerated. The words "communicate" and "community" come from a Latin root which means "common." To communicate is *to impart, to share, to make common* one's thoughts, feelings and questions. As noted in *Human Communication and Its Disorders* "... the function we call language involves a system of communication among persons who have grouped themselves together and therefore developed a community wherein certain symbols — both verbal and visual — possess arbitrary conventional meanings."

Not only is communication the key to entrance into the community; it is also the force which binds people together in a culture. Persons who are unable to communicate are only weakly bonded to the culture and they are forced to exist as fringe members of their community. Learned dependence is often observed in children who cannot express their ideas, describe their feelings or ask questions. They settle into the role of a passive recipient of care. Many exhibit the behavior patterns of an egocentric child who, as Piaget noted, seems to show a lack of concern with being understood. The more mature child, functioning at the sociocentric level, "addresses his hearer, considers his point of view, tries to influence him or actually exchanges ideas with him." Communities are composed of persons who are predominantly sociocentric. To function at this level one must be able to communicate.

In a community, most communication takes place through speaking and listening. Some children are unable to develop intelligible speech but can understand the speech of others. They must learn how to use another method of communication if they are to mature and function effectively in human society. For some, writing can be developed as an expressive mode but learning to write legibly is often impossible for physically handicapped children who have poor control of arms and hands. There are other children whose difficulty with symbols which are referenced to the sounds of language is manifested in speaking, reading and writing. It is not within the compass of this chapter to identify and discuss the various etiologies of speech, reading and writing disorders. Our intent is to observe that many children are unable to develop the basic skills of speaking, reading and writing to the level of social utility. Unless they acquire early another mode of communication, the children are likely to suffer stunted cognitive and social-emotional growth. They will be forced to exist on the outer edge of their community because they lack the primary means of social interaction: communication. Since 1971 many handicapped persons — including some who functioned at low cognitive levels — have learned to communicate with Bliss symbols when they could not learn to speak intelligibly or to read traditional orthography.

The search for universal language

Bliss symbols were not developed with the problem of communicatively handicapped persons in mind. Bliss was trying to fulfill humanity's long-time wish for a universal language. It is estimated that more than 3000 languages are spoken in the world. Each is complex and, when used by a speaker and listener familiar with the language, allows for a great variety of expressions and permits fine shading of meanings. To one who does not understand the language, however, the utterances are meaningless. Interactions between nations, as in diplomacy and commerce, are often impeded by a language barrier.

It is estimated that 700 artificial languages have been proposed over the centuries. As early as 1629, Descartes outlined a language in which numbers were used to represent words and ideas. Only two of the artificial languages have received much attention, Volapuk and Esperanto. Volapuk (which means ''world's speech'') was invented in 1880 by Johann Schleyer, a Roman Catholic priest. The vocabulary consisted of English and Romance words which were phonologically simplified. While it enjoyed early support, its popularity declined because it was too difficult for non-linguists and because of competition from Esperanto, which was more easily learned. Ludwig Zamenhof's description of Esperanto was published in 1887 under the pseudonym ''Dr. Esperanto'' (which means ''one who hopes''). The vocabulary consists of words common to major European languages. Speech sounds peculiar to one language are eliminated. The spelling is phonetic and uses twenty-one consonants, two semivowels and five vowels. Esperanto has been the most successful of the artificial languages. Several million people are able to speak Esperanto, and it has been used in writing books and journals, and for translation of books from other languages. Although it has been used at international conferences, Esperanto has not become a truly universal language.

Some experts argue that a "natural" language rather than an "artificial" language might more easily become accepted as an interlanguage. Basic English was designed between 1926 and 1930 by two British linguists, C. K. Ogden and I. A. Richards. Basic — B(ritish) A(merican) S(cientific) I(nternational) C(ommercial) English — consists of 850 words, of which 600 are names of things or events (nouns), 150 are names of qualities or properties (adjectives) and 100 are operational words. In addition to the basic vocabulary, special classes of words needed by, for example, the sciences, have increased the vocabulary to about 8000 items. There have been similar attempts to create Basic French, Basic Russian, Basic Chinese and Basic Spanish.

It is to be noted that Volapuk, Esperanto and Basic English are sound referenced; that is, the symbols represent sounds made in speaking a word that stands for an object or event. Each of these languages has a phonology and an orthography. As will be discussed in detail in a later section, Bliss symbols are meaning referenced with no phonetic associations.

Development of Bliss symbols

Karl Blitz was born in 1897 in Austria near the Russian border, where many nationalities lived in close proximity. As a child he observed that "different nationalities hated each other because they spoke and thought in different languages." After graduating as a chemical engineer from Vienna University of Technology he entered an electronics firm and eventually became chief of the patent department. Again he noted the problems caused by "patent specifications in vague and ambiguous words of different languages." When Hitler overran Austria in 1938, Blitz was sent to a concentration camp where he saw people killed "all because of words." He was freed because he "softened the hearts" of his jailers by entertaining them with music played on instruments smuggled to him by his wife, Claire. He fled to England, where he changed his name to Charles Bliss. He worked in a London factory until he left for Shanghai to be reunited with Claire on Christmas Eve, 1940. She had made her way there from Germany through Russia and China.

In Shanghai, Bliss was influenced by Chinese symbols. The ideographic writing made it possible for many peoples, each of which spoke a different language, to unite, because their leaders could read the symbols regardless of the language spoken. In 1942 he began developing pictorial symbols. In 1943 he was interned in Shanghai by the Japanese. After the war he and his wife emigrated to Australia. Here he worked in an automobile assembly plant, but devoted all available time to library research, study and development of his symbol system and writing. In 1949 he published *Semantography*. Unable to find a publisher, he typed the manuscript on stencils and his wife duplicated them. The 700 pages were bound in three volumes, which constituted the first edition of *Semantography*. About three years later the typewritten pages were reproduced by the photo-offset process to become the 882-page second edition. An "enlarged" second edition was published by the same process in 1965.

Following completion of the first edition, Bliss entered on a campaign of letter writing and other activities designed to inform universities, libraries, professors and educators about his symbols and to recruit their support. Although over 6000 letters were sent, few were answered and fewer orders for the volume were received. A few scholars, such as biologist Julian Huxley and philosopher Bertrand Russell, responded favorably, but generally his work was ignored. Naturally, Bliss was bitterly disappointed that his symbols did not receive recognition and acceptance, a condition which prevailed until they were "discovered" in 1971 by Shirley McNaughton of the Ontario Crippled Children's Centre.

Bliss, as he explains in *Semantography* (1965, p.10), wanted to do more than devise a universal language. It was his vision to develop a writing that:

1. can be read in all languages;
2. can give literacy to all;
3. can expose illogic and lies;
4. can demask the demagogues;
5. contains a simple semantics and logic which even children can use for their problems;
6. contains a universal ethics without religious legends, and acceptable to all;
7. can unite our world, so disastrously divided by languages, legends and lies.

It is important to understand that Bliss did not anticipate that his symbols would be used by communicatively handicapped persons, including many who function at a low cognitive level. Adapting Blissymbolics, which was developed for mature and sophisticated language users, to the needs of communicatively handicapped persons has necessitated some revisions of and additions to the symbols and symbol system. Such work was initiated at the Ontario Crippled Children's Centre in Toronto, Ontario, Canada.

Early history of the use of Bliss symbols with handicapped children

The Ontario Crippled Children's Centre initiated a symbol communication program in September 1971 with the object of developing "a system of communication which would serve as a complement to or substitute to speech for the pre-reading child." The SCP (Symbol Communication Project) staff felt that, while picture boards enable children to communicate about immediate needs, pictures are inadequate for expressing more complex thoughts and feelings; hence, non-speaking children are restricted to low levels of communication until they learn to read and can use word boards. An interdisciplinary team was formed, which sought to develop a communication system to "bridge the gap between pictures and words." Since many non-speaking children also have difficulty in pointing because of poor control of hands and arms, the team decided to focus also on developing a system that could be displayed in a form suitable for use with electro-mechanical signalling devices.

Initially, selected children at the Ontario Crippled Children's Centre (OCCC) were taught symbols designed by the SCP team. In October 1971, Shirley McNaughton, a special education teacher at OCCC, came upon a description of Bliss symbols in Elizabeth Helfman's *Signs and Symbols Around the World* and a short time later obtained a copy of the 1965 edition of *Semantography* from Laurentian University in Sudbury, Ontario. Beginning in the fall of 1971, the SCP staff concentrated on using Bliss symbols, at first taking symbols directly from *Semantography*. Since, as noted previously, Bliss had not anticipated the use of his symbols by handicapped children, many symbols needed by young, physically handicapped children were not to be found in *Semantography*. New symbols based on the Bliss system were created by the SCP staff. Bliss visited OCCC in May 1972 to revise and improve some of the newly developed symbols and he returned periodically for conferences and discussions. Through 1974 the use of Bliss symbols was refined and expanded at OCCC. Vocabularies were developed, assessment procedures described, and electro-mechanical devices designed and constructed.

By 1975, interest in Bliss symbols was widespread and handicapped children in widely separated centers were learning to use Bliss symbols — now "Blissymbols." Application of the symbol system was spreading rapidly and broadly.

Purpose and activities of the Blissymbolics Communication Foundation

In July 1975, through the support of the Ontario Crippled Children's Centre, the Blissymbolics Communication Foundation was established as a non-profit, charitable organization. Through a legal agreement with Charles K. Bliss, the Foundation received a *perpetual, exclusive, world-wide* license to the copyright on Blissymbolics. The agreement also provided for continuing consultation from Mr. Bliss on the creation of new symbols.

Several important developments occurred in 1978. The name of the Blissymbolics Communication Foundation (BCF) was changed to the Blissymbolics Communication Institute (BCI). The word *Foundation* suggested that a fund or endowment was available to maintain the Blissymbolics Program and to finance projects in education and research. Actually, no funds were available to support the work of BCF other than those received as grants for specific projects and the income from training programs and sale of materials. A widely used meaning of *Institute* is "an institution for advanced study, research and instruction in a restricted field." Institutes must seek funds to carry on their work. The organizational structure of the Blissymbolics program is more accurately described as an *Institute* rather than a *Foundation*. (The purposes and activities of the Blissymbolics Communication Institute are described in Appendix A.)

A second major event of 1978 was publication of *The Handbook of Blissymbolics for Instructors, Users, Parents and Administrators*. Also in 1978, symbol stamps and grids became available to facilitate the construction of individualized symbol displays for symbol users. (The Handbook and symbol stamps are described in Appendix A.)

In 1980, *Blissymbols for Use* was published by BCI. This book contains 1400 symbols with their English equivalents, arranged both by symbol structure and symbol meaning.

Clearly the development of Blissymbolics as a communication mode for communicatively handicapped persons has progressed rapidly since the 1971 beginning at the Ontario Crippled Children's Centre. As do all new educational methodologies, Blissymbolics will trigger many studies. Careful research is needed, for at the time of this writing, only a little is known about how communicatively handicapped children learn symbols, what symbols they need to learn, and how they should be taught. It is to be hoped that researchers and clinical observers realize that for their investigations to be meaningful they must *know* the symbols and *understand* the symbol system. Many hours of careful study of Blissymbolics and practice in the use of Blissymbols should be prerequisite to their application in research or teaching.

When I first read about Blissymbols in *Time* magazine, my quick reaction was that the symbols were a curiosity and a fad and wouldn't be around for very long. Following a meeting at the Ontario Crippled Children's Centre with members of the original Symbol Communication Project Staff, my attitude changed from rejection of the idea to skepticism about the possible value of Blissymbols as a communication mode for children who cannot learn to speak or write. During 1975, the Trace Center conducted a series of national workshops on non-vocal communication techniques and aids in which Shirley McNaughton and I participated. While listening to Ms. McNaughton's discussion of Blissymbolics I was impressed by several aspects of Blissymbolics of which I had not been aware earlier:

1. Except for a few arbitrary symbols (most of which are in general use) symbols are based on a rationale which, if understood, facilitates interpretation and retention of their meaning.

2. Symbols can be used generatively, i.e., by following simple drawing rules and keeping in mind the rationale on which individual symbols are based, new symbols with new meanings can be created by combining two or more symbols.

3. Symbols are meaning referenced and, hence, can be interpreted without reference to sounds or words. The significance of this characteristic of Blissymbols became clear when I learned that symbol messages written by children in Montreal who spoke no English could be interpreted readily by children in Toronto who understood no French. How this is possible is explained below. First study the French, German, Greek and English word lists and then study the list of Blissymbols.

FRENCH	GERMAN	GREEK	ENGLISH	BLISS
sentiment	Ruhrung	αἴσθημα	feeling	♡
heureux	glückselig	χαρούμενος	happy	♡↑
triste	traurig	λυπημένος	sad	♡↓

FRENCH	GERMAN	GREEK	ENGLISH	BLISS
orgueilleux	stolz	ὑπερήφανος	proud	♡⌄—.
fâché	zornig	θυμωμένος	angry	×♡⌄《

Each of the lists contains words relating to feelings. In the French, German, Greek and English lists, the reader gets no clue from the symbol as to its meaning. Each word is phonetic based and the characters or letters refer to sounds made when the word is pronounced. Translating one word in the list provides no assistance in translating the others. In the Blissymbolics list,

the heart symbol ♡ which means *feeling*, appears in all the other symbols; hence, we know that each of the symbols refers to a feeling. Study the other parts of each Blissymbol and note that each part gives a meaning-referenced clue to the feeling intended:

happy (feeling up) note direction of arrow
sad (feeling down) note direction of arrow
proud (feeling superior) note position of dot
angry (much feeling of opposition) note multiplication sign and direction of arrowheads

A speaker of any of the above languages could think, in his own language, about a feeling. If he spoke the word for the feeling, persons not knowing his language would not understand him. But if the feeling were expressed in Blissymbols it could be interpreted by a speaker of any language, because the symbols are referenced to meaning, which remains the same regardless of language. This feature — meaning referencing — makes Blissymbols a powerful communication tool and one that may be easily learned and remembered.

II. Blissymbolics

There is much more to Blissymbolics than a set of graphic symbols. There is a rationale on which each symbol is based. There are rules for drawing symbols to preserve their form and meaning. There is a logical basis for putting symbols together to make new symbols. A simple grammar and syntax provide many forms for expressing meaning. Bliss originally referred to his work as *Semantography*, from the Greek words *semanticos* (significant meaning) and *graphein* (to write); hence, "to write meaning." This term proved to be too general, so the term *Blissymbolics* was adopted to distinguish the system from other methods of "writing meaning." Bliss describes Blissymbolics as "a new kind of shorthand which can be read in all languages. It contains also a simple logic, semantics and even ethics." (*Semantography*, p.8) In this chapter we will discuss the system of Blissymbolics: the "shorthand," the logic and the semantics. I recommend that you read Bliss' interesting views on language and ethics, which he discusses in the publications listed in the Bibliography.

The Nature of Blissymbols

By a "symbol" Bliss means some sign you can point at which has meaning (*Semantography*, p.567). By using, in various combinations, some basic symbol elements, Bliss has designed what he regards as a "complete pictorial symbol language." Bliss stresses that "a pictorial symbol, a picture and a word for it, cannot tell all there is contained in the meaning." What does a symbol mean? Bliss says, "A symbol . . . means what we agree it should mean." (*The Book to the Film 'Mr. Symbol Man,'* p.33) A key word in this statement is "agree." Clearly if different persons attach different meanings to the same symbol or use different symbols for the same meaning, communication cannot take place. To maintain uniformity of symbol drawings and symbol meaning, the symbols have been copyrighted. In symbol displays developed by BCI, the symbol Ⓑ is used to indicate a symbol which differs from the C. K. Bliss version either in symbol form or in the words used to denote meaning of the symbol.

Bliss stresses that no symbol is self-explanatory. In his view it would be impossible to develop a pictorial symbol writing that "could be read right away without any explanation.'' The meanings of symbols must be learned; however, ''learning is easy and simple when the symbols show the outlines of the real things we want to picture and symbolize.'' (*The Book to the Film 'Mr. Symbol Man,'* p.49) An important characteristic of Blissymbols is that they are *meaning referenced* rather than sound referenced. Each visual symbol represents a thing, an action, an evaluation or an abstract meaning. Printed words — though visual — represent sounds which make up the acoustic symbol for a thing, an action, an evaluation or an abstract meaning.

Symbols are composed from a relatively small number of forms which Bliss calls ''symbol elements.'' Following a logical system, these basic elements are used in various combinations to represent thousands of meanings. Symbols are of several types:

1. Pictographs

Drawings that resemble what they are intended to symbolize:

house	flag	book	animal

2. Arbitrary symbols

Drawings that have no pictorial relationship between the form and what they are intended to symbolize. The word ''arbitrary'' is usually defined as ''determined by will or caprice; selected at random; based on no thought-out reason.'' Blissymbols are probably not ''arbitrary'' in this dictionary sense.

a, an	the	that	this

Some arbitrary symbols are already in wide use:

1 2 3 4 5 6 7 8 9 0

+ − × ÷ ⹀ · ?

Bliss calls the following ''arbitrary symbols of semantography'' (*Semantography* p.118) but he gives a *reasoned* explanation for each:

☐   "chemical THING . . . outline of the most symmetrical, beautiful form of crystal, already formed at a time, when the hardening earth crust was in utter chaos." (*Semantography*, p.107)

∧   "physical ACTION . . . indicates in its outline one of the most primeval ACTIONS on earth, the forming of volcanic cones and the thrusting up of mountains." (*Semantography*, p.107)

∨   "human EVALUATION . . . the outline of a cone, standing on its top, indicating a very labile position. The cone may instantly topple over when pushed, and it takes a lot of balancing to keep it in this precarious position. Just as with many EVALUATIONS of ours, which we hold, and which topple over, when challenged." (*Semantography*, p.108)

)("TIME . . . the outline of two parabolic mirrors, the one turned backwards to mirror the *past*, the other turned forward to focus the *future*. In between past and future is the *present*, a fleeting glance, a moment." (*Semantography*, p.107)

△   NATURE, CREATION In *Semantography*, p.108, Bliss writes, "This symbol is wholly arbitrary, and we may say, that man shall ever use only an arbitrary symbol for this meaning. He can grasp the universe with his mind and the limitations of his mind will limit his grasp of this meaning."

However, in *The Book to the Film 'Mr. Symbol Man,'* p.35, he notes two derivations of the symbol. In the Greek search for divine order and harmony in the world they found it in the crystals that showed beautiful and harmonious forms. This led to the study of geometry and the view that the most harmonious and simplest geometrical figure is the equal-sided triangle. He also arrives at the symbol in "a more modern way" by using the symbol for *earth* ___ which represents matter, in combination with the symbol for *action* ∧ which represents energy, to form △ which represents *creation* and creator.

3. Ideographs

Drawings that symbolize the idea of a thing rather than the name of it. An ideograph creates a graphic association between the symbol and the concept it represents:

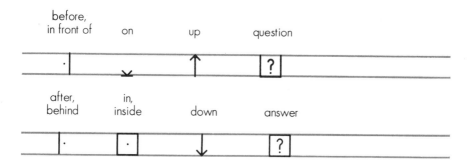

4. Compound symbols

Groups of symbols arranged to represent objects or ideas:

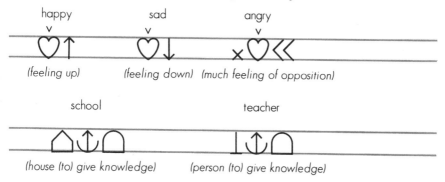

In the graphic sense, Blissymbols are line drawings which conform to standards established by Charles K. Bliss and the Blissymbolics Communication Institute. In the semantic sense, Blissymbols represent people, things, actions, feelings, relationships and ideas.

Importance of the square

Since the meaning of a symbol depends on *size, position* and *spacing*, as well as on the *configuration* of the drawing, it is necessary to have a frame of reference to which differences in size and position and spacing may be related. The form to which all symbols must bear specified size and position relationships is the *square*. The square might be of any size, but only symbols based on a square of the same size can be used together. The base of the square is at the *earthline* and the top of the square at the *skyline*.

Symbol size, position and spacing are further determined by dividing this large square into smaller squares, thus giving horizontal and vertical guidelines for determining the position of symbols. The area subdivisions also aid in determining size. In this way symbols of different sizes are kept proportional to each other. Of course, the subdivided square does not appear in a symbol message or in a vocabulary list.

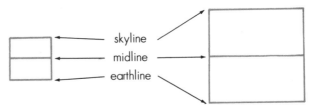

The *earthline* is a horizontal reference line always on the bottom of the square. The *skyline* is an identical horizontal reference line but always on the top of the square. As we shall see, many symbols are referenced to the earthline and the skyline. The horizontal midline is also an important referent for positioning certain symbols.

Factors that determine symbol meanings

1. Configuration

Configuration, or shape of the symbol, is an important indicator of intended meaning. Even what might appear to be a slight change in configuration alters the meaning of the symbol, as illustrated in the following examples.

A horizontal line drawn the full length of the baseline of the square represents the *earth:*

By changing the shape of the symbol through shortening the line to one half the baseline and drawing a vertical line from the center of the line to the top of the square (the *skyline*) we create the symbol for *person:*

The symbol for *man* combines the half-sized Blissymbol for *action* with the upper half of the *person* symbol:

Only a small change in the configuration distinguishes the symbol for *man* from the symbol for *woman:*

which contains the half-sized Blissymbol for *creation*   plus the upper half of the symbol for *person*. The shape of the symbol for *house* is pictographic:

Note that the roof is a full square horizontally, a half square vertically and the apex is located at the midpoint of the skyline. This roof configuration represents the concept of *protection* and appears in many other symbols:

parent	father	mother
(The person who provides protection)	*(The man who provides protection)*	*(The woman who provides protection)*

2. Size

Size must be considered when interpreting the meaning of a symbol, since some configurations are used in more than one size. Three sizes are used in drawing Blissymbols: full size, half size and quarter size. A full-sized circle, that is, one whose circumference would touch the sides of the square we have taken as our frame of reference, symbolizes the *sun*. A half-sized circle centered between the earthline and skyline is the symbol for *mouth*:

sun   mouth

A few symbols appear in the three sizes; for example, the symbol element

∧   when drawn full size means *the action*; in half size ∧   it means *activity* and in quarter size it is placed above another symbol to denote *making action:*

The action	activity	action indicator

When drawn full size, the square represents an *enclosure*; a half-sized square means *thing*, and the quarter-sized square when placed above another symbol, is a *thing indicator:*

The symbol ╳ when drawn full-size means *multiplication*; in half size (with the symbol for evaluation) ╳̌ it means *much, many,* and in quarter size, placed above another symbol, it is the *plural indicator:*

3. Position

Position or location within the frame of reference, the square, carries meaning in the case of certain symbols. As already noted, a horizontal line drawn along the base of the square means *earth*, while one drawn along the top of the square means *sky*. The same line drawn along the horizontal midline of the square means *subtraction:*

A half-sized plus sign drawn on the baseline denotes *belongs to*; when drawn in the middle of the square it means *and* or *also*. The same form drawn on the skyline means *with the help of:*

4. Direction

Direction of symbol parts and/or the *orientation* of features of certain symbols determine their meaning. This factor is noted particularly in the use of what Bliss calls ''the versatile arrow symbol'' (*The Book to the Film 'Mr. Symbol Man,'* p.48).

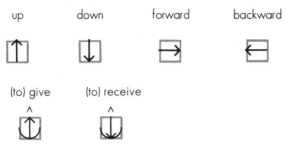

up	down	forward	backward

(to) give	(to) receive

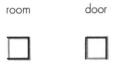

The square drawn with only three sides completed has different meanings depending on the orientation of the opening:

room	door

The meaning of a slanted line is determined by its orientation:

a, an	the

5. Spacing

Spacing between parts of a symbol may carry the meaning, as in the following symbols:

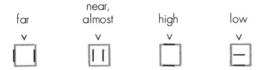

far	near, almost	high	low

6. Pointer

A *pointer* (in earlier BCI publications called the *location indicator;* see BCI *Bulletin* III: 1, p.7) is used to direct attention to a detail of a symbol and thus that detail becomes the intended meaning. The pointer is drawn as a right angle and has the appearance of an arrowhead. When a pointer is used with a symbol for a body part and might appear to create a new shape, the pointer is located one-eighth space from the symbol (see the symbol for *foot* below). In other symbols the pointer touches the symbol, as in *floor* and *wall* below:

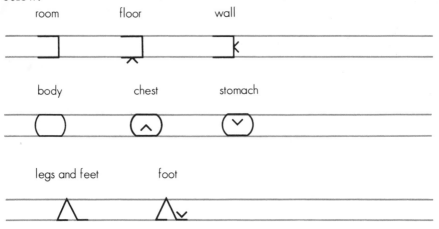

room   floor   wall

body   chest   stomach

legs and feet   foot

7. Number

A *number* used with a symbol alters or makes more specific the intended meaning of the symbol, as in the symbolizing of personal pronouns:

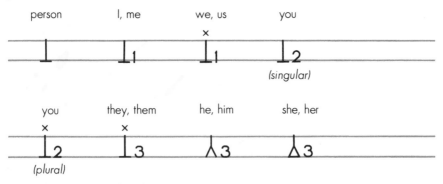

person   I, me   we, us   you

(singular)

you   they, them   he, him   she, her

(plural)

Day of the week is specified by placing the appropriate number following the symbol for day:

Sunday   Monday   Tuesday

8. Positional referents

Positional referents may be used to give meaning to a symbol. In this case the symbol consists of two or more components, one of which functions as the referent. It is the positional relationship of the referent to the other component which determines the meaning. For example in the symbol

the enclosure symbol is the referent. Since the dot is *in* the enclosure, the symbol means *in* or *inside*. In the symbol   . the dot is outside the enclosure; hence, the symbol means *out* or *outside*. Following are other examples:

over   under

(to) come   (to) end, stop   (to) start, begin

Positional referents are not to be confused with position, a factor discussed earlier. Position refers to location within the frame of reference, the square. In interpreting position, we note whether the symbol is drawn on the earthline, the midline or the skyline. In interpreting *positional referents*, we note the spatial relationship of one symbol part to another.

9. Compound and combined symbols

Meanings may be represented by grouping two or more symbols. Each of the symbols, when drawn alone, has a recognized meaning. In the group, the individual symbols contribute to a new meaning. Two types of grouping are used: compound and combined.

A *compound symbol* is a symbol grouping created by C. K. Bliss, or one which has been accepted into the standard vocabulary developed by BCI. As illustrated in the examples below, in some compound symbols the individual symbols are superimposed; in other compound symbols the individual symbols are sequenced.

Superimposed compound symbols

1.

⊥   drawn alone means *person*

∧   drawn alone means *protection*

⬆   when the two symbols are superimposed in this manner, the new symbol means *parent*, the person who provides protection

2.

⊢   drawn alone means *chair*

∿   drawn alone means *water, liquid*

⊢∿   when the two symbols are superimposed in this manner, the new symbol means *toilet*, chair over water

3.

⊗   when drawn alone means *wheel*

⊢   when drawn alone means *chair*

⊠   when the two symbols are superimposed in this manner, the new symbol means *wheelchair*

4.

∿   when drawn alone means *water, liquid*

↓   when drawn alone means *down*

↓∿   when superimposed in this manner, the new symbol means *rain*, water coming down

Sequenced compound symbols

1.

♡   when drawn alone means *feeling*

↑   when drawn alone means *up*

♡↑   when the two symbols are sequenced in this manner, the new symbol means *happy*, feeling up

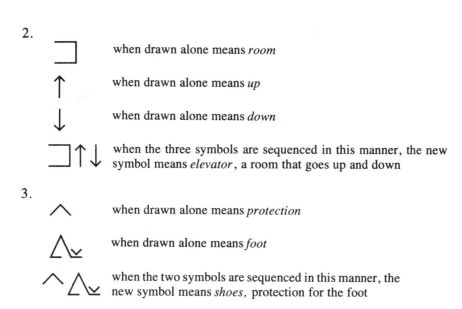

2.

      when drawn alone means *room*

      when drawn alone means *up*

      when drawn alone means *down*

      when the three symbols are sequenced in this manner, the new symbol means *elevator*, a room that goes up and down

3.

      when drawn alone means *protection*

      when drawn alone means *foot*

      when the two symbols are sequenced in this manner, the new symbol means *shoes,* protection for the foot

A *combined symbol* is a grouping invented by a user or instructor for personal use only. Components of a combined symbol must be sequenced; they may not be superimposed. Combined symbols must always be enclosed between *combine indicators*. Placing the *combine indicator before* AND *after* the sequence of symbol units not only delimits the symbols that are being grouped but also indicates that the combination is not to be regarded as an approved Blissymbol but rather as a symbol created by the user for a specific communicative situation. Following is an example of a combined symbol developed by symbol users for a specific situation.

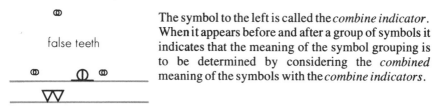

false teeth

The symbol to the left is called the *combine indicator*. When it appears before and after a group of symbols it indicates that the meaning of the symbol grouping is to be determined by considering the *combined* meaning of the symbols with the *combine indicators*.

Explanation of components of above combined symbol:

      teeth — a pictograph

      make believe — to be in the clouds, above the sky

Rules and guidelines for creating and recording a combined symbol will be discussed later in this chapter. At this time it is important only to understand the difference between a *compound* and a *combined* symbol. The combined symbol is similar to the sequenced compound symbol except that the latter was developed by C. K. Bliss or the BCI and has been accepted into the standard symbol vocabulary, whereas the combined symbol is developed for a specific situation by a symbol user or instructor.

Indicators and their use

It is to be noted that C. K. Bliss regards the grammar of most languages as "illogical." He wrote (*Handbook of Blissymbolics* Appendix 1, *Syntax Supplement*, pp. 235–250), "When I was a child my logical sense was so strong that I simply refused to learn the irregularities of the grammar imposed on me." He has sought to make a grammar which is simple and logical. He wants to " . . . do away with the nightmares of irregular verbs." Bliss regards adjectives as "the worst of words" (*The Book to the Film 'Mr. Symbol Man,' p.99)*, because " . . . they belong to the inner world of our mind. And if we give them a negative meaning we can get into deep trouble with ourselves and our fellowman." With his view toward grammar it is not surprising that Bliss would abandon the traditional parts of speech. The reader will be tempted to interpret Bliss' indicators in the terms customarily employed when parsing a sentence; however, it is to be understood that Bliss did not intend that the indicators be synonymous with or identical to the traditional parts of speech. Following is a description of the indicators. Note that indicators are quarter-sized shapes and are always drawn one-quarter space above the skyline. When used with a single symbol, the indicator is centered over the symbol. Rules for placement of the indicator in compound and combined symbols will be discussed later.

1. Thing indicator

A quarter-size square, derived from the Blissymbol for *thing*, placed one-quarter square above the skyline, indicates that the symbol represented is a chemical THING.

Bliss says that it is simple to find out whether a word means a real THING. Ask these questions:

Can we see it?

Can we photograph it?

Can we touch it, if we can get near enough?

Can we put it on a scale and weigh it, provided we have a scale big enough? (*The Book to the Film 'Mr. Symbol Man,'* p.56)

People, objects and animals are chemical THINGS. While chemical things are nouns, it is difficult to define a "noun." In English, nouns are traditionally defined as words naming a person, place or thing but nouns also name actions, qualities and ideas. Nouns have many forms and grammarians have devised numerous schemes for defining nouns. Bliss' classification of THING is similar to but not synonymous with the English noun.

In BCI practice the *thing indicator* is not used with all symbols for things (nouns). Generally "noun" symbols are unmarked; however, when a symbol might have both an abstract and a concrete meaning, the *thing indicator* is used with the concrete meaning, as in the following example:

time   clock

(abstract)   (concrete)

Bliss notes that THINGS perform ACTIONS and he says that it is easy to determine whether a word means a real action:

Find the THING that performs the ACTION.

We can photograph the THING and its ACTION with a movie camera.

(*The Book to the Film 'Mr. Symbol Man,'* p.56)

The reader will observe that, in English, verbs are traditionally defined as words which express *action* and, in this way, Bliss' ACTION classification is similar to the English verb. However, Bliss proposes to simplify verb forms to actions occurring in the *present, past,* or *future.* Symbolizing distinctions of time when an action occurred is essential for accurate communication.

2. Action indicator

A quarter-sized version of the full-sized symbol that denotes *The action* placed above a symbol indicates action taking place in the present.

3. Past action indicator

A quarter-sized version of the full-sized symbol that means *past*, means 'make action in the past' when placed above the appropriate symbol. The symbol is an outline of a parabolic mirror facing backward and thus "mirroring the past." (*Semantography*, p.317)

4. Future action indicator

To specify action in time yet to come the parabolic mirror faces forward and is thus "focusing on the future." (*Semantography*, p.317)

5. Description (evaluation) indicator

Bliss notes that apart from the words indicating chemical THINGS and physical ACTIONS, we have a third group of words which indicate human EVALUATIONS. They usually indicate meanings that we don't find in nature but only in our heads. Earlier we discussed Bliss' remarks on this symbol: it is precariously balanced on its point; its position might be changed easily and so it is with human evaluations. What we describe as "good" today may appear "bad" tomorrow. Nevertheless it is often necessary to describe THINGS as happy, sad, angry, afraid, etc., or ACTIONS as being performed early, late, quickly, slowly, etc. Proper placement of the symbol ˅ over another symbol shows that a descriptive term based on a human judgment or evaluation is the intended meaning.

6. Plural indicator

Things may exist individually or as more than one. In English this change in number is indicated in various ways: adding "s" (cow – cows), adding "es" (cross – crosses), adding "en" (ox – oxen) or changing a vowel (foot – feet). Some words use the same form for singular and plural (deer – deer; sheep – sheep). In Blissymbolics more than one of a THING is specified by placing a quarter-sized symbol for *multiplication* ✕ above the appropriate symbol.

Following are illustrations of how indicators change the meaning of a symbol:

mind	minds	brain	thoughtful
	×	□	v
⌒	⌒	⌒	⌒
	PLURAL	THING	EVALUATION

think	thought	will think
∧	)	(
⌒	⌒	⌒
ACTION PRESENT	ACTION PAST	ACTION FUTURE

Extended meanings of symbols

A single symbol, depending on the semantic context in which it occurs, may be translated into different words. This is an important feature of Blissymbols and, in part, is a result of the parsimony ("economy in use of specific means to an end" or, Why have many symbols when one symbol will communicate the thought?) of the Bliss system. C. K. Bliss makes frequent use of this feature and in *Semantography* often gives several meanings for a symbol. For example, he gives as possible meanings of ◯̂ *to speak, report, say, tell, narrate.* Funk and Wagnalls *Standard Handbook of Synonyms* lists *"say," "tell"* and *"talk"* as synonyms of *"speak"* and gives *"narrate"* as a synonym for *"report."* Clearly these meanings are interrelated. In Blissymbolics these words are represented by the same symbol.

There is not yet agreement on a standard term for this feature of Blissymbols. "Range of meaning" has been used in lectures and communications. "Range" might seem to suggest the spread from highest rank to lowest rank and "range of meaning" might be interpreted as implying that the meanings have been ranked on some characteristic. Obviously there has been no such ranking of the meanings given to a symbol.

Even though one might think of some arguments against considering the several meanings of a symbol as synonyms, we find the following definition of *synonym* as it appears in *Webster's New International Dictionary* helpful in understanding the multiple meanings of a Blissymbol:

> **Synonym:** One of two or more words of the same language having the same or nearly the same meaning. . . . Synonyms are words which express what is the same idea but which differ from one another in some shade of meaning, in emphasis, or, especially, in their connotation.

Following are some examples of symbols with multiple meanings:

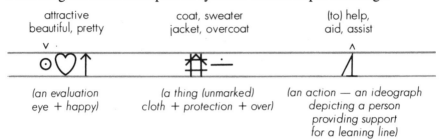

attractive beautiful, pretty	coat, sweater jacket, overcoat	(to) help, aid, assist
(an evaluation eye + happy)	(a thing (unmarked) cloth + protection + over)	(an action — an ideograph depicting a person providing support for a leaning line)

Because of space constraints it is not possible to give all possible meanings of a symbol on a communication board or other symbol display; however, in a few cases two words appear with a symbol. They may represent a different level of sophistication in vocabulary or two related but not synonymous meanings associated with the basic concept.

boat, ship	car, vehicle	near, almost

When communicating with a sophisticated symbol user it may be necessary for the receiver of the message to suggest or inquire about synonyms instead of interpreting the symbol only in terms of the displayed meaning. Bliss suggests to users of *Semantography* (pp.829–830) ''Use with this book and this dictionary index also a book on synonyms and antonyms. . . . When you can't find a word look it up in the Thesaurus and find the similar meanings which are listed there. Then look up the corresponding symbol.'' He notes that joy may occur with the ''discovery that so many words in English, and in other languages, can be expressed by one or two basic symbols.'' The BCI publication, *Blissymbols for Use*, provides several synonyms for the most commonly used English equivalent in most of its symbol entries. These synonyms can also be found in the Index at the back of the book.

Additional symbols for a working vocabulary

The index of symbolized meanings in *Semantography* lists hundreds of meanings which one can express by using various combinations of basic symbol elements. Additional symbols are being developed by BCI to meet the needs of handicapped persons. It is not the purpose of this text to describe all the currently available Blissymbols. Rather, our focus will be on developing a beginning vocabulary for persons who cannot speak intelligibly; however, some higher level lexical items will be introduced as we demonstrate how the system operates.

1. Body parts

The parts of the body are represented by pictographs. In the drawing at the left below we can find the symbols for *eye, ear, nose* and *mouth*. And the drawing of the "little man" incorporates a number of body parts.

Below are symbols for several parts of the body to which frequent reference is made:

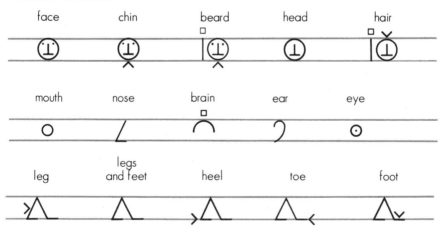

Note that when used with body parts the pointer does not touch the other symbol element; it is separated by one-eighth space:

body	neck	shoulder	chest

stomach	breast	crotch	waist

2. Feelings

The heart shape ♡ appears an an element in the compound symbols which are used for expressing feelings and emotion. While recognizing that the heart is not the seat of emotions, Bliss notes that "... many millions of people in many lands have for many centuries used the word 'heart' to express emotionally our 'heartfelt' love, our 'heartiest' wishes, from 'the bottom of our heart' ... etc." For this reason he chose the

heart shape ♡ as a basic symbol (*The Book to the Film 'Mr. Symbol Man,'* p.92). Bliss presents symbols for the expression of many types of feelings. Children commonly want to communicate that they are happy, sad, angry, upset, afraid, and sometimes, proud. Here are the symbols for those emotions:

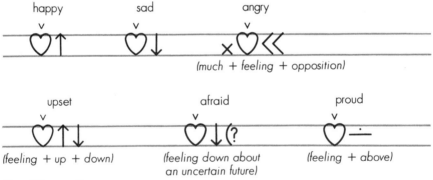

happy   sad   angry
(much + feeling + opposition)

upset   afraid   proud
(feeling + up + down)   (feeling down about an uncertain future)   (feeling + above)

3. People

Earlier in this chapter the following symbols for people were presented:

person   man   woman   father   mother

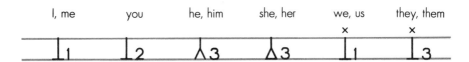

I, me	you	he, him	she, her	we, us	they, them

Careful study of the following compound symbols will show that the symbol for *person, man* or *woman* is an element in all symbols representing adults:

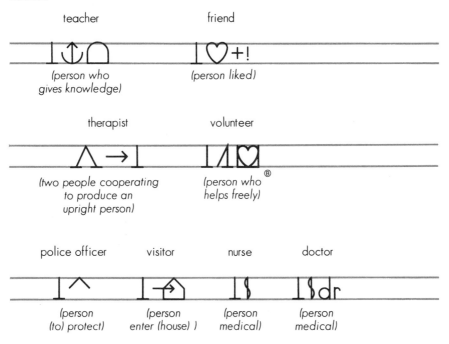

teacher
(person who gives knowledge)

friend
(person liked)

therapist
(two people cooperating to produce an upright person)

volunteer
(person who helps freely)

police officer
(person (to) protect)

visitor
(person enter (house))

nurse
(person medical)

doctor
(person medical)

Symbols for members of the family are of special interest and usefulness to non-speaking children. Careful study of the following compound symbols will show that they are formed by arranging in various ways two or more of these symbol elements:

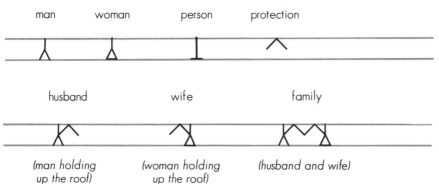

man   woman   person   protection

husband
(man holding up the roof)

wife
(woman holding up the roof)

family
(husband and wife)

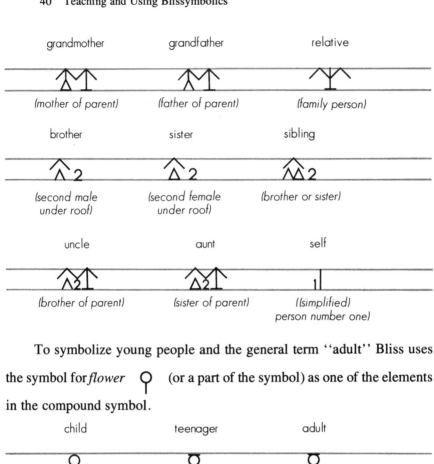

grandmother	grandfather	relative
(mother of parent)	(father of parent)	(family person)

brother	sister	sibling
(second male under roof)	(second female under roof)	(brother or sister)

uncle	aunt	self
(brother of parent)	(sister of parent)	((simplified) person number one)

To symbolize young people and the general term "adult" Bliss uses the symbol for *flower* ♀ (or a part of the symbol) as one of the elements in the compound symbol.

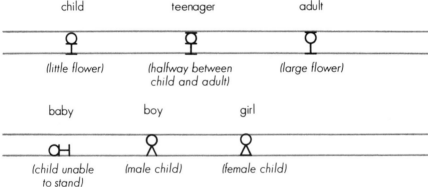

child	teenager	adult
(little flower)	(halfway between child and adult)	(large flower)

baby	boy	girl
(child unable to stand)	(male child)	(female child)

4. Food

The basic symbol for food ○ represents what the *mouth* ○ receives from the *earth* ——— . In this superimposed compound, the earthline is shortened to half size. The *food* symbol appears in other symbols that represent certain types of food:

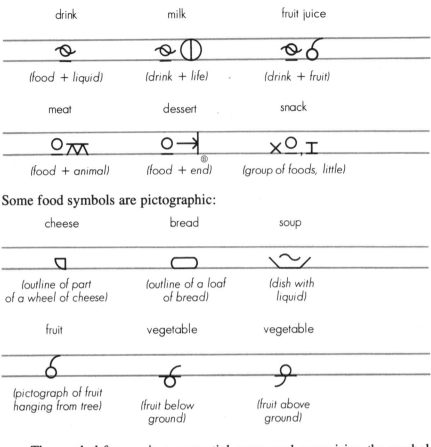

drink	milk	fruit juice
(food + liquid)	(drink + life)	(drink + fruit)
meat	dessert	snack
(food + animal)	(food + end)	(group of foods, little)

Some food symbols are pictographic:

cheese	bread	soup
(outline of part of a wheel of cheese)	(outline of a loaf of bread)	(dish with liquid)
fruit	vegetable	vegetable
(pictograph of fruit hanging from tree)	(fruit below ground)	(fruit above ground)

The symbol for *egg* is a sequential compound comprising the symbol for *seed* and the symbol for *life*:

seed	life	egg

Bliss explains that the symbol for *life* combines the symbol for *sun* and the symbol for *individual*. We "live on this planet by the energy which is coming daily to us from our *sun*." (*Semantography*, p.410)

To meet children's needs for a symbol to represent one of their favorite foods, BCI developed the following sequential compound for *hamburger* using the symbols for *roll* and *meat*:

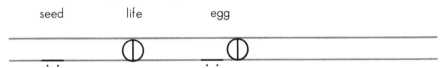

roll	meat	hamburger

5. Clothing

The pictographic symbol for *cloth* ⊞ (woven fabric) and the symbol for *protection* ∧ appear in many of the compound symbols that represent articles of clothing:

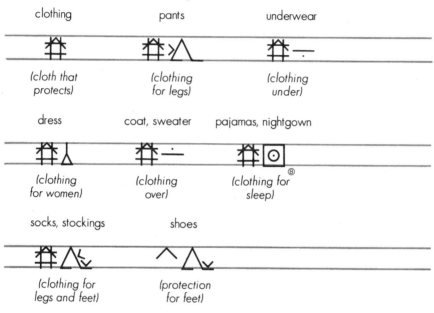

clothing	pants	underwear
(cloth that protects)	(clothing for legs)	(clothing under)

dress	coat, sweater	pajamas, nightgown
(clothing for women)	(clothing over)	(clothing for sleep)

socks, stockings	shoes	
(clothing for legs and feet)	(protection for feet)	

The symbols for *bandage* and *accessory* also contain the symbol for *cloth:*

bandage	accessory
(cloth + protection + medical)	(thing added to clothing)

Particles

A particle is a grammatical form that is used to show syntactical relationships. Particles are short words that have no inflection; that is, their form cannot be changed to create different grammatical or syntactical relationships. Whereas the form of nouns and pronouns may be changed to indicate number, gender and case and the form of verbs changed to indicate tense, the form of particles is invariant. *Prepositions, conjunctions* and *interjections* are classified as particles. Some sources also include articles in this category. The following definitions from *Webster's New World Dictionary of the American Language* (Second College Edition, 1974), provide a quick review of these parts of speech.

1. Conjunction

An uninflected word used to connect words, phrases, clauses, or sentences. Conjunctions may be:

(a) coordinate (e.g., and, but, or)
(b) subordinate (e.g., if, when, as, because, through)
(c) correlative (e.g., either . . . or, both . . . and)

2. Preposition

A relation or function word, as in English "in," "by," "for," "with," "to," etc., that connects . . . a noun or pronoun, or a syntactic construction, to another element of the sentence, as to a verb: (he went *to* the store), to a noun: (the sound *of* loud music), or to an adjective (good *for* her).

3. Interjection

An exclamation thrown in without grammatical connection, such as "ah!" "ouch!" "well!". The *American Heritage Dictionary of the English Language* defines an interjection as "A part of speech consisting of exclamatory words capable of standing alone; for example, oh!"

In *Semantography* (pp. 420–450) and in *The Book to the Film 'Mr. Symbol Man'* (pp.88–89), Bliss discusses the particles of speech as "Anarchy in Language." Noting that particles comprise about forty per cent of our speech and writing, he stresses that there is great potential for misunderstanding because of the ambiguity of many frequently used particles. For example, does the phrase, "The books *of* Smith" refer to books Smith owns or books he has written? Many particles have idiomatic uses. The expression, "I'll call you *up*" does not mean the opposite of "I'll call you *down*." Bliss argues that particles are "shorthand" words for "big" words. Determination of the "big" word meaning clarifies the meaning of the "shorthand" word (i.e., the particle). It is from the symbol for the "big" word meaning that Bliss derives the symbol for the particle. For example, consider "addition" to be the big word — or the basic concept. Words such as "and," "also," "too," which are particles, convey the notion of "in addition to." The symbol for addition is a full-sized

╋ . The particles derived from the concept (big word) *addition* are represented by a half-sized ╼╋ drawn on the horizontal midline. Symbols for the particles are derived from the symbol for the "big" word. They are reduced in scale and sometimes simplified as illustrated below:

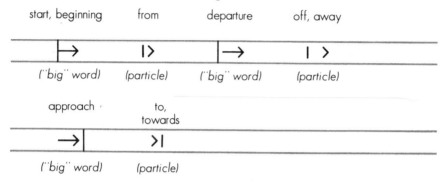

start, beginning	from	departure	off, away
("big" word)	(particle)	("big" word)	(particle)

approach	to, towards		
("big" word)	(particle)		

The symbols for the particles *at, here* and *there* are derived from the symbol for *position* ⟩. which Bliss defines as "the indication of a *relation* to a certain *point* in space." This concept of *relationship* also appears in the *Webster's Dictionary* definition: "the place where a person or thing is, especially in relation to others." To express *position* Bliss uses the mathematical symbol for *relation* ⟩ and adds . (dot).

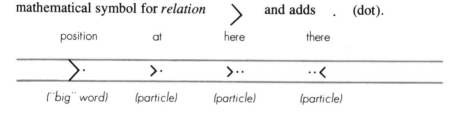

position	at	here	there
("big" word)	(particle)	(particle)	(particle)

By setting the dot where it does not indicate a position because, in Bliss' words, "we have not yet decided where to place it," symbols for the particles *either* and *or* are derived:

either	or

The symbol for *relation* also appears in the symbol for *purpose*, which is the "big" word meaning from which the particle *for* is derived. Bliss noted in *Semantography* (p.433) that purpose involves a relationship: "we do something in relation to something else to achieve a certain purpose." To stress the special relationship which would fulfill the purpose the *relation* symbol is repeated:

purpose	for
$\gg$	$\gg$
("big" word)	(particle)

counter-purpose	against
$\ll$	$\ll$
("big" word)	(particle)

Bliss cautions that the symbol $\gg$ should not be used to represent some of the idiomatic uses of the word "for." When "for" is used to indicate *exchange* as in the phrase "three *for* a dollar," it means "three in exchange for a dollar." To represent this meaning of the word "for" he derives $\overset{\wedge}{\underset{\vee}{}}$ *for* (in exchange for) from $\overset{\wedge}{\updownarrow}$, the symbol for *(to) exchange*.

Concerning the particle "of," Bliss wrote in *Semantography* (p.427): "If you ask me, what was the most difficult word to translate into a symbol, I answer: the most difficult problem arises because *of* has so many meanings." *Webster's New International Dictionary* lists twenty meanings for the particle "of" (e.g., "from," "belonging to," "with," "concerning," "on," "before") each of which is semantically different from the others. Confusing uses of the particle "of" are found in many languages. For accuracy in communication one should be careful when using the word "of" particularly when communicating with persons unfamiliar with the idiomatic uses of the word. The following symbols, derived from the symbol for the "big" word meaning *relation*, indicate how Bliss expresses two common uses of the particle "of."

of, about	of, by
$>$	$<$

Bliss includes *what, why, which, where, when, who,* and *how* with the particles. (In the BCI stamps these words are not listed with the particles but in a section of special symbols for changing meaning or asking questions.)

The derivation of the symbols for these particles is explained below. Note that each particle except *where* is represented by a sequential compound with the   ?   appearing as the first element.

what

?

Bliss uses the question mark as the symbol for *what*

what thing

?□

When the question mark is followed by a symbol for *thing*, the meaning is *what thing*

who

?⌐

what person

which

?÷

what division

why

?▷

what cause (Bliss derives the symbol for *cause* ▷ from the symbol for *relation* ⟩ and describes cause in relation to an effect)

cause   effect

▷   ⅀

wedge   imprint

when

?🕒

what time (Time is represented by the ideograph based on a clock face)

where

?

what place (Simplified from the sequential compound which means *what place*)

?⌄

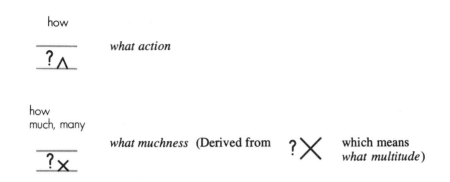

how

———
? ∧   *what action*

how
much, many

———
? ×   *what muchness* (Derived from ? ⤬ which means
                                                         what multitude)

The following additional symbols are included with the particles in the BCI stamps:

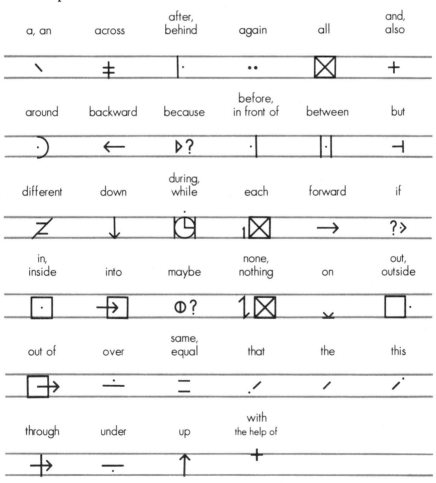

a, an	across	after, behind	again	all	and, also
＼	╪	·┃	··	⊠	+

around	backward	because	before, in front of	between	but
·)	←	▷?	·┃	┃·┃	⊣

different	down	during, while	each	forward	if
⨅	↓	◔	₁⊠	→	?>

in, inside	into	maybe	none, nothing	on	out, outside
▯·	⇥	Ⓞ?	1⊠	⌄	▯·

out of	over	same, equal	that	the	this
▭⇨	÷	＝	⟋·	⟋	⟋·

through	under	up	with the help of		
⇥	⎯·	↑	+̣		

III. Techniques for Changing Symbol Meaning

We have seen how *indicators* can be used to change the meaning of a symbol, as illustrated below:

feeling	heart	(to) feel	felt
	□	^	)
♡	♡	♡	♡

will feel	feelingly	feelings	hearts
(	v	×	□×
♡	♡	♡	♡

The effect of indicators is to change the grammatical form of the word symbolized. We have also seen how *pointers* change the meaning of a symbol to a specific part of the thing symbolized:

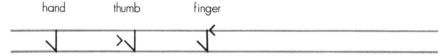

hand   thumb   finger

Indicators and pointers are so important to symbol meaning that they are incorporated into many of the symbols printed in the BCI stamps. The symbol with an indicator or pointer has a conventional meaning.

Bliss has described several techniques by which a symbol user can indicate that he intends a different meaning from the conventional translation of a symbol. Symbol users and symbol instructors have developed additional techniques. To facilitate use of these techniques, a 3 x 6 inch cell grid is included with the symbol stamps. This grid, which is headed *My Special Blissymbols*, is designed for grouping those symbols which the user employs to indicate that the word printed above a following symbol does not represent the intended meaning. Rather, the preceding ''special symbol'' indicates how the following symbol is to be interpreted.

The techniques for changing symbol meanings, which these ''special

Blissymbols'' represent, have been called ''strategies.'' This may not, however, be the best term to use as a classifier for these meaning-changing techniques. The term ''strategy'' suggests a *plan*, which is a broader concept than a technique. Strategies are usually directed toward achieving a long-range objective. While some strategies are used in the *permanent approved* symbols (*cold* is symbolized as the *opposite meaning* of *hot*:

drawer is symbolized as *part of* a chest of drawers: ⠂÷⠂ ▦), special

meaning - changing symbols are often used on a *temporary* basis to create a word for a particular message. Perhaps it would have been better to classify these procedures as *tactics,* which *Webster's New Dictionary* defines as ''any methods used to gain an end; especially, skillful methods or procedures.'' Tactics, as distinguished from strategies, are directed toward short-range objectives. Our interest in changing the meaning of a word is short-range — it is intended that the new meaning will be used only in a specific instance. Perhaps an operational description such as ''meaning-changing techniques'' will clarify the purpose of the ''strategies'' described and illustrated in the following pages.

1. Opposite meaning

Bliss derives the symbol ↥ for *opposite meaning* from *up and down*

and comments (*Semantography*, p.245) that this symbol ''will help us express many words.'' It is to be noted that this symbol does not mean *opposite* as in the sentence ''The boy sat *opposite* (i.e., across from) the girl''. Rather it signals the intended expression of an antithetical thought, for example:

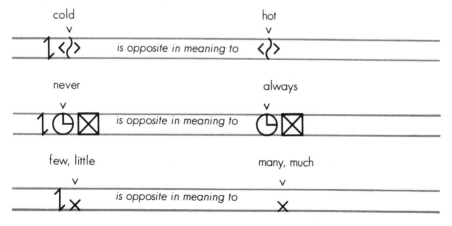

empty   full
v   v

	is opposite in meaning to	

2. Part (of)

Bliss points out that in all languages there are words that express a part of something else (*Semantography*, pp. 250–251). For example flame is a part of fire, drop is a part of liquid, branch is a part of tree. Rather than create a separate symbol for these parts, their meaning may be specified by using the half-sized division symbol ∸ before another symbol, to indicate that we want to refer to only *a part of what the succeeding symbol means*.

flame   fire

	is a part of	

word   language

	is a part of	

drop   water, liquid

	is a part of	

branch   tree

	is a part of	

3. Metaphor

Bliss discusses metaphor several places in *Semantography*. He notes (p.552) that "a metaphor may be found sometimes a useful instrument to convey a difficult meaning" but generally he expresses concern about the dangers inherent in the wide use of metaphors in speaking and writing. Particularly he is distressed that citizens are often deceived and misled by the metaphorical language of their politicians. So deep is his concern about the dangers in metaphors that he likens his symbol for *metaphor* to a warning signal, similar in appearance to a warning sign used on the railroads and highways. The symbol is a superimposed compound formed from ⊥

person and ◯ *mouth*. Its use signals that the reader should not translate the following symbols literally but rather as a figure of speech.

Webster's New World Dictionary defines metaphor as a "figure of speech containing an implied comparison, in which a word or phrase ordinarily used of one thing is applied to another," for example, the word "plows" in "The ship plows the sea." In rhetoric the metaphor is regarded as the most basic of all figures of speech. A metaphor states an analogy, similarity or relation between two things. Bliss seems to view the meaning of metaphor more broadly and its use in changing symbols meanings follows this broader interpretation.

Persons using Blissymbols for communication can change the meaning of a group of symbols by placing the metaphor symbol a full space before the group of symbols.

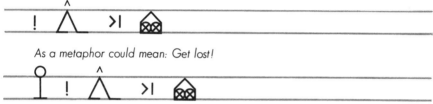

4. Intensity

Bliss makes frequent use of the exclamation mark in deriving symbols. This symbol ❘ when placed a quarter space *after* the symbol it modifies,

acts as an intensifier. This is a good term, since it signals that a stronger or more vivid concept is intended than that represented by the original symbol, as indicated in the following examples:

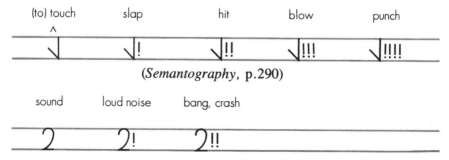

(*Semantography*, p.288)

Symbol users and symbol instructors have developed additional ways of changing symbol meanings. It is to be noted that these strategies are not a part of the original Bliss system; however, they have proved useful in helping non-speaking persons express themselves.

5. Symbol part

By using the symbol for *Blissymbol* followed by the symbol for *part* a symbol user can create a symbol with which to indicate that only part of a following symbol is to be translated:

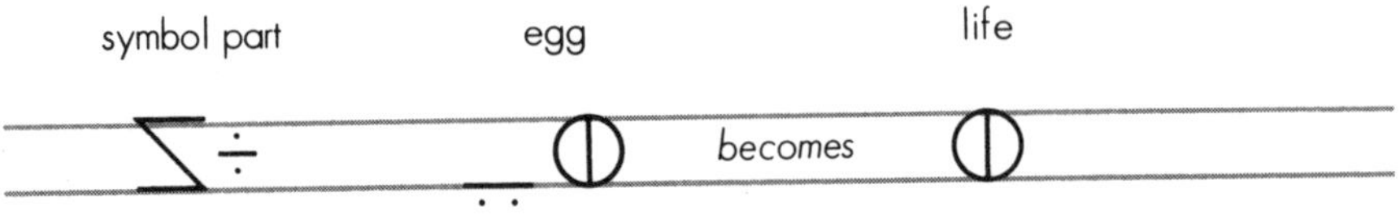
symbol part
egg
life
becomes

This strategy should not be confused with *part (of)* as in

fire
flame
which becomes

where *flame* is a *part of fire* and the strategy calls attention to *part of a thing* rather than *part of a symbol*.

6. Similar (to)

By sequencing the symbol for *near* and the symbol for *equal* Bliss has derived a symbol which expresses such concepts as *near equal, like, as, similar*. He does not include it with his techniques for changing the meaning of a symbol or group of symbols; however, symbol users have employed this strategy when a symbol for the word they want to express is not available, as in the following example:

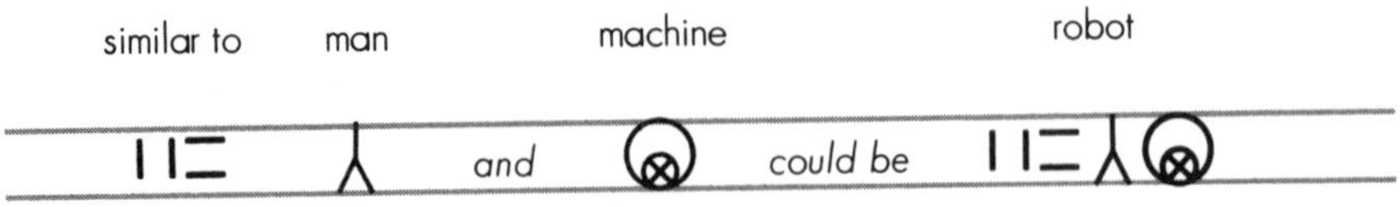
similar to
man
machine
robot
and
could be

7. Similar sound

In English there are words that are pronounced the same, that is, they *sound like* each other but have different meanings, for example: *bear* and *bare*, *flower* and *flour*. Such words are called "homonyms." In the absence of a symbol for *flour* a symbol user might use the symbol $||\overline{=}2$ to indicate that a word which *sounds like* flower is intended:

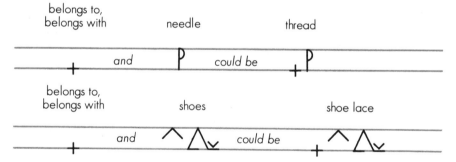

Obviously this strategy would not succeed when communicating with a speaker of another language whose words for *flower* and *flour* would not be homynyms.

8. Belongs to, belongs with

This strategy employs the symbol ____ which, drawn on the earthline, means *belongs to*. As used by Bliss, *belongs to* denotes possession. Symbol users have broadened the meaning to indicate that one thing belongs with another thing as thread belongs with a needle:

belongs to, belongs with		needle		thread
$+$	and	ρ	could be	$+$ρ

belongs to, belongs with		shoes		shoe lace
$+$	and	⋀⋀	could be	$+$⋀⋀

9. Letters of the alphabet

When a user's symbol display lacks a symbol for identifying a specific meaning within a class, the user can clarify his intended meaning by using a letter of the alphabet with the symbol:

animal				dog
⋀⋀	and	d	could be	⋀⋀d

boy   Robert

⊗   and   **R**   could be   ⊗**R**

city   Philadelphia

××⌂   and   **P**   could be   ××⌂**P**

10. Combining symbols

Earlier we discussed *combined symbols* and distinguished them from the *sequential compound symbol*. Whereas combined symbols are created by a symbol user for a specific situation, the sequential compound symbol is created by C. K. Bliss or is one accepted into the standard BCI vocabulary. It was noted that *combine indicators* ⅏ are not used with a compound symbol but that they must be placed *before* and *after* the symbols grouped into a combined symbol.

In the hands of a symbol user with sufficient cognitive development and creativity, combining symbols can be a powerful technique for expressing a meaning when a precise symbol is not available. BCI has developed the following guidelines for creating combined symbols:

1. Aim for conciseness, transmitting only the essential meaning element.
2. The most important element, called the *classifier*, is usually placed first in the sequence.
3. Modifying symbols usually *follow* the classifier sequentially, except the following, which precede the classifier:

   much/many   part (of)   minus/without
   opposite meaning   similar

Following are some examples of combined symbols. Note that the most important element — the classifier — appears first in the sequence.

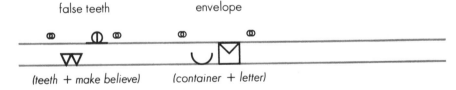

false teeth   envelope

(teeth + make believe)   (container + letter)

11. The negative

Symbol meaning may be changed by placing the *negative symbol* —| a full square before the symbol whose meaning is to be altered. The symbol —| means *not* and is derived from _ *minus* and | *intensity*. It should not be confused with —|| which means *no* and is derived from —| *not* with | *intensity*. Note in these examples that use of the negative *sometimes, but not always*, results in a meaning similar to that obtained through the use of the special symbol *opposite meaning* ∿ .

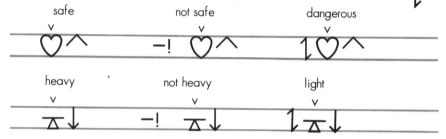

12. The possessive

In English there are many ways of showing possession: 's as in "the boy's books," s' as in "the boys' books," "of" as in "the books of the boys," and change in the form of pronouns (my, mine, your, yours, his, hers, its, our, ours, their, theirs, whose). Bliss denotes possession through the use of the symbol ═╪═ drawn half-size on the earthline. (He observes that this symbol resembles a tombstone and quips that this resemblance should remind us that "you can't take it with you!") Placing this symbol *one-quarter space after* a noun or pronoun changes that noun or pronoun to the possessive form:

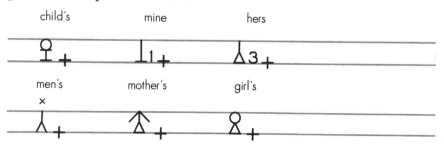

This use of ‾‾‾‾‾‾ is not to be confused with its use in the strategy _belongs to, belongs with_. When _belongs to_ ‾‾‾‾‾‾ is used as a technique to change meaning, the symbol is placed _one-quarter space before_ the symbol to which it refers.

13. Classifiers

The intended meaning of a Blissymbol can be clarified by the use of a symbol that indicates the class or category into which the associated symbols fall. Interpreted alone, the symbols have individual meanings, but when interpreted as being members of the _class_ specified by the _classifier_, the meaning assigned must fall within the _class_ specified. To illustrate, ⌐ means _chair_, ⌐⌐ means _table_. When preceded (as shown below) by the classifier ♀ which means _generalization_, the _grouping_ is to be interpreted as _furniture_. In _Semantography_ (p.548), Bliss writes that the symbol for _generalization_ expresses "a saying about a multitude."

furniture

BCI, in response to the requests of teachers and pupils, devised a symbol for _sex_ which combines part (but not all) of the _male_ symbol and the _female_ symbol preceded by the _generalization_ symbol.

sex

Below are three other classifiers: _linear thing, material_ and _chemical product:_

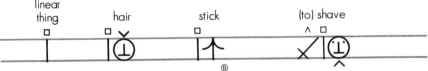

| linear thing | hair | stick | (to) shave |

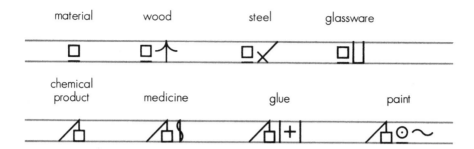

14. The relativizer

We have presented and discussed the symbols Bliss developed for the following words when they are used as interrogatives: "who," "which," "when" and "where", as in:

Who is that man?   *Where* are you going?
Which one do you want?   *When* will you return?

These words may be used also as relative pronouns or as subordinate conjunctions, as in the following sentences:

1. The man *who* came to visit is my uncle.
2. The pencil, *which* is broken, is mine.
3. The house *where* I live is near a lake.
4. I will call you *when* I have the answer.

To symbolize these words when used in a non-interrogatory way, Bliss employs quotation marks drawn on the horizontal midline:

,,

This symbol is called the *relativizer*. The same symbol is used for many relative pronouns and subordinate conjunctions. The word into which the symbol is translated is determined by the semantic context in which it occurs, for example:

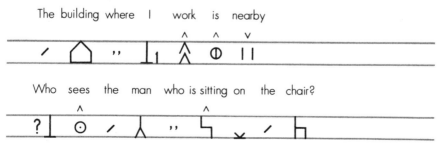

It is to be noted that the *relativizer* is not interchangeable with the symbols employed in interrogative sentences. The word *who* in the sentence above is represented by two symbols: **?⊥** at the beginning of the sentence, where it denotes interrogation, and **,,** for the relative pronoun which opens the subordinate clause.

15. Evaluation before and evaluation after an action

Bliss stresses that the word ''can'' involves a human evaluation which is made *before* an action, and in some instances may be incorrect. One might say, ''I can jump over a house,'' when in reality one cannot jump over a house. He symbolizes the verbs *can, (to) be able* in this manner:

> ∧
> ·∨
>
> The half-sized evaluation symbol is *preceded* by a dot which indicates that the evaluation was made *before* the action.

Many modifiers involve evaluations made *before* or *after* an action. To symbolize such words, which function as adjectives, Bliss places the quarter-sized symbol for *evaluation*, with an appropriately placed dot, over other symbols, as in the following examples (*Semantography*, p.378; *The Book to the Film 'Mr. Symbol Man,'* p.108).

BEFORE THE FACT	AFTER THE FACT
breakable	broken
·v	v·
⌐\	⌐\
wettable	wet
·v	v·
∼	∼
washable	washed
·v	v·
♡	♡
mortal	dead
·v	v·
∅	∅

16. Big meaning — little meaning

Several words may have similar connotations; that is, they express notions that are similar but not identical. This characteristic of words is explained in Bliss's discussion of "(to) possess" and "(to) have." He notes that these phrases sometimes refer to an earthly (material) thing rather than to a spiritual thing; hence, he derives his symbol for *(to) possess* from the symbol for *earth* and the symbol for *addition*. *Possess* suggests outright ownership, so the symbol elements are drawn full size. The verb "(to) have" does not signify outright ownership but "stands between this and temporary ownership. It has a 'smaller' meaning and this is indicated by minimizing the symbol for ownership" (*Semantography*, p.367). In the symbol for *(to) have* the elements are drawn one-half size:

Another illustration of *big* meaning – *little* meaning is shown is the following symbols:

IV. Bliss Syntax

Linguists have identified several levels of language:

Phonological level. The sounds of speech which, when appropriately sequenced, form words. There is no counterpart in Blissymbolics to the phonological elements of language, that is, to the speech sounds. Blissymbols are all meaning referenced rather than sound referenced.

Morpholigical level. Those changes in words which create a new meaning. The smallest meaningful unit in a language is the morpheme. In the sentence, "The girls undressed their dolls and carefully put the dresses in boxes" the morphemes are: the, girl, s, un, dress, ed, their, doll, s, and, care, ful, ly, put, the, dress, es, in, box, es. In this sentence morphemes have changed number from singular to plural, tense from present to past and nouns to modifiers. In Blissymbolics such changes are made through the use of indicators and other meaning-changing techniques.

Syntactic level. The order of words to produce grammatically correct sentences. In English and most other languages many syntactic forms are used. The various languages use different word orders to express the same meaning. Bliss has developed a syntax which he feels is simple yet adequate to express the most sophisticated and complex thoughts.

Semantic level. The meaning carried by the words as they have been arranged in a particular order. The title "Semantography" indicates that Bliss was more concerned about *meaning* than *form*. In Blissymbolics, form is not employed for stylistic reasons but as a way to express meaning.

The term "grammar" is used to mean the *rules* of phonology, morphology and syntax. A grammar is essential for effective communication. In his *Syntax Supplement* (*Handbook of Blissymbolics*, Appendix 1) Bliss commented that it took years to develop the grammar of his symbol system. During these years he was developing and typing other parts of the system and, as a result, he wrote, "chapters on a universal grammar are interspersed between hundreds of pages [in *Semantography*] and difficult to find for any serious student of my symbol language." In this chapter we will describe the word order proposed by Bliss for different types of sentences: statements, negative statements, enlarged sentences, commands, statements of possibility, questions, negative questions and passive voice sentences. The reader will note that some of the structural forms used by Bliss employ word orders that are different from those used in English.

Some symbol instructors report feeling uncomfortable about teaching these forms because the word order is not what the child hears speakers use. Also, questions have been raised about the possible effect of using these forms upon the learning and use of English syntax. While there are important questions to be investigated, it is important to note that Bliss' intention has been to *simplify* grammar to the minimum essential for clarity of expression. As he wrote in *Semantography* (p.315), ''The grammar of semantography is not intended for learning a foreign tongue. It is solely constructed as a simple device for the people, who can speak their mother tongue (no matter how 'incorrect'), but who need some rules to construct internationally valid sentences in semantography.''

As indicated in the following diagram, there are several possible interactions of things and persons:

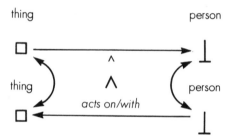

1. Statement forms

These interactions make possible four statement forms in Bliss syntax:

1. *Thing act on/with thing*

(The) animal   drinks   water.

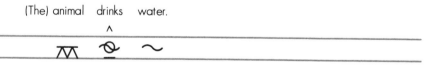

Note: The correct syntax of ''thing acts on thing'' could be obtained with ''water drinks animal,'' which is not semantically meaningful; therefore, it is essential that symbol users apply a test of meaningfulness to the statement formulated.

2. *Thing act on/with person*

(The) telephone surprised   him.

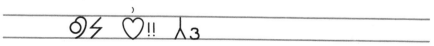

3. *Person act on/with person*

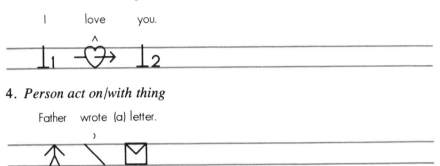

4. *Person act on/with thing*

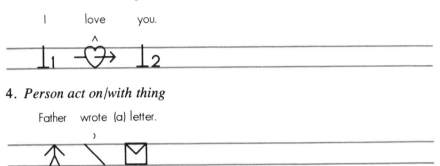

2. Enlarged sentences

Children at an early age begin to expand their utterances beyond the simple statement forms and most adult communication employs sentences consisting of many words. In *Semantography* (p.316) Bliss sets forth a specific word order for enlarged sentences that contain information about *place* and *time*. At the beginning of the sentence the *place* is indicated, followed by *time*, which is in turn followed by the remainder of the sentence, as illustrated below:

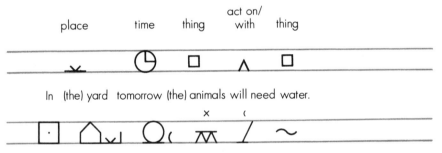

In both written and spoken English the word order would be:

The animals in the yard will need water tomorrow.

Both word orders convey the same message. In *Semantography* Bliss gives no rationale for mentioning *place* and *time* at the beginning of the sentence except to note that "Mentioning the time at the beginning of the sentence makes it unnecessary to indicate the . . . tense of the verb." (p.316) Omission of the tense indicator might follow logically from this Bliss word order, but for persons learning to communicate the omission might be confusing. On the other hand, some beginning communicators are aided in getting their message across if they are asked to indicate first when and where something took place or is to take place, e.g., "Thursday at the circus I saw a bear."

3. Negative statements

In negative statements the symbol for negative is placed *before the verb*:

Father won't be writing (a) letter.

(The) animal   doesn't need   water.

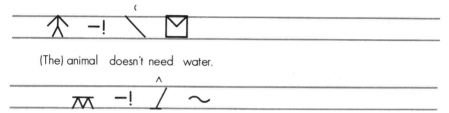

4. Command form

Imperative sentences, that is, statement forms that issue commands, are punctuated in English by placing an exclamation mark (!) at the end of the sentence. In Bliss syntax the command symbol is placed at the *beginning* of the sentence:

Sit!

Stop (the) work!

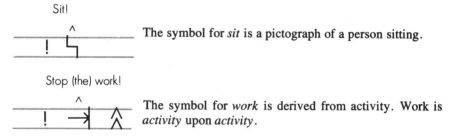

The symbol for *sit* is a pictograph of a person sitting.

The symbol for *work* is derived from activity. Work is *activity* upon *activity*.

5. Polite command form

In English grammar, softened or polite commands are expressed in phrases that differ from those used in direct commands: ''courtesy'' words are used, and the exclamation point omitted at the end of the sentence, for example:

Please think no more of it.

Suppose we say nothing more about it.

In Bliss syntax, the polite form follows the word order: *please action*. Since the symbol for *please* is a sequential compound,   the exclamation mark appears at the opening of the sentence as in the direct command. The command is softened or made polite by the meaning of 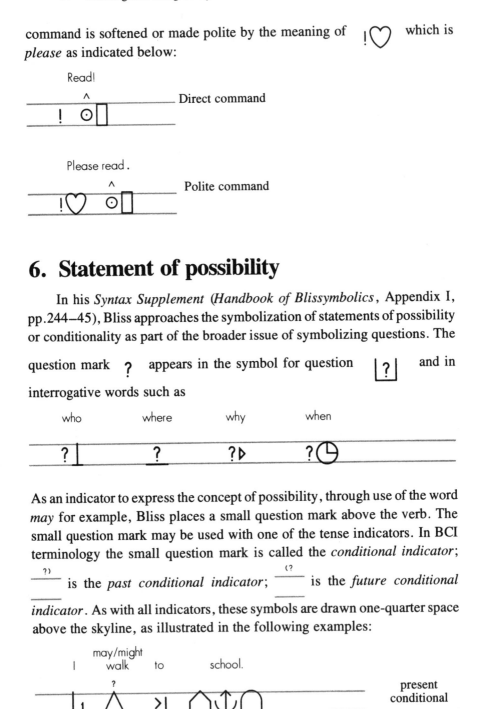 which is *please* as indicated below:

Read!

— Direct command

Please read .

— Polite command

6. Statement of possibility

In his *Syntax Supplement* (*Handbook of Blissymbolics*, Appendix I, pp.244–45), Bliss approaches the symbolization of statements of possibility or conditionality as part of the broader issue of symbolizing questions. The

question mark ? appears in the symbol for question and in interrogative words such as

who   where   why   when

As an indicator to express the concept of possibility, through use of the word *may* for example, Bliss places a small question mark above the verb. The small question mark may be used with one of the tense indicators. In BCI terminology the small question mark is called the *conditional indicator*; is the *past conditional indicator*; is the *future conditional indicator*. As with all indicators, these symbols are drawn one-quarter space above the skyline, as illustrated in the following examples:

may/might
walk   to   school.

present conditional

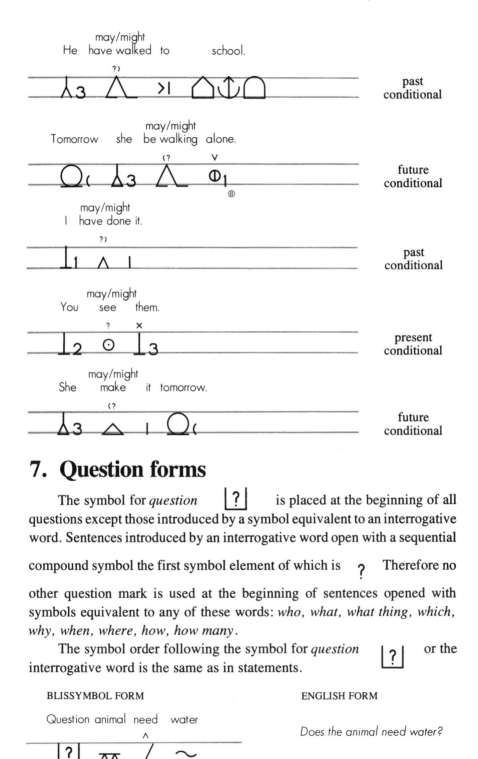

may/might
He   have walked to   school.

?)

past
conditional

may/might
Tomorrow   she   be walking alone.

(?   v

future
conditional

may/might
I   have done it.

?)

past
conditional

may/might
You   see   them.

?   x

present
conditional

may/might
She   make   it tomorrow.

(?

future
conditional

7. Question forms

The symbol for *question*   ⌐?⌐   is placed at the beginning of all questions except those introduced by a symbol equivalent to an interrogative word. Sentences introduced by an interrogative word open with a sequential compound symbol the first symbol element of which is   ?   Therefore no other question mark is used at the beginning of sentences opened with symbols equivalent to any of these words: *who, what, what thing, which, why, when, where, how, how many*.

The symbol order following the symbol for *question*   ⌐?⌐   or the interrogative word is the same as in statements.

BLISSYMBOL FORM   ENGLISH FORM

Question animal need   water

Does the animal need water?

∧

⌐?⌐ ⋔ / ∼

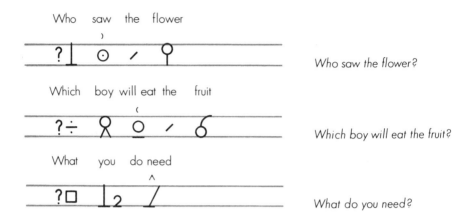

8. Negative question

The symbol order for a negative question is the same as the symbol order for a negative statement, in that the symbol for the negative $-|$ is placed before the verb. Note in the following examples that, as with all questions, the symbol for question $\boxed{?}$ is placed at the beginning of the sentence.

BLISSYMBOL FORM   ENGLISH FORM

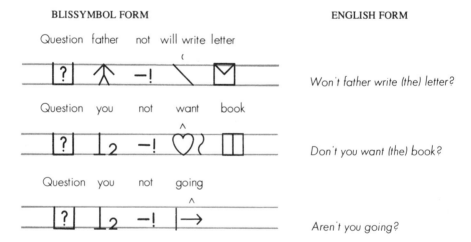

9. Passive voice

So far all of the sentences given in this section on syntax have been in the active voice; that is, the subject has been the *doer* of the action indicated by the verb. Bliss recommends (*Semantography*, pp.320–321) that we "use only the active form, the natural order, that is the order of cause and effect.'' He advises the communicator against indulging ''in complicated sentences and in subtle differences of expression.'' He shows how to write the passive form in symbols ''for the critics . . . who may think that the passive form is a problem too difficult for semantography.'' The procedure is simple: write the sentence in symbols with the subject as *receiver* of action and place the action symbol above the verb *but with the point toward the subject.*

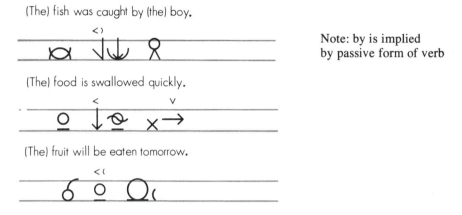

(The) fish was caught by (the) boy.

Note: by is implied
by passive form of verb

(The) food is swallowed quickly.

(The) fruit will be eaten tomorrow.

10. Unessential words

Repeatedly in *Semantography* Bliss advises symbol users ''not to use long sentences in semantography'' and to use simple rather than cumbersome grammatical constructions. For example, he contends that ''I was'' conveys the same meaning as ''I have been'' or ''I had been.'' Also he stresses that particles might often be omitted without sacrificing meaning; for example, ''I'll meet you four o'clock'' means the same as ''I'll meet you *at* four o'clock.'' ''I need pencil'' conveys the same thought as ''I need *a* pencil''. Blissymbolics includes symbols for the so-called function words (i.e., words that carry relatively little independent meaning but perform a grammatical function); however, when writing sentences in symbols, Bliss omits function words except when they are essential for correct interpretation of meaning. Some symbol instructors liken this to *telegraphic style*, a term referring to writing in which many function words (especially articles and connectives) are omitted. Since the cost of a telegram is based on the number of words transmitted, telegraphic messages are short, concise and terse. Shortness, conciseness and terseness are also characteristics of sentences written in Bliss syntax. The shortness of Bliss sentences, however, results not from a deliberate attempt to limit the number of words in a message but from the use of a simple grammar and the avoidance of ambiguous and evaluative words. When evaluative words are used they are marked to show that they represent a ''human evaluation'' rather than a physical thing or a physical action. For these reasons the term *telegraphic style* is probably not an accurate description of sentences written according to Bliss guidelines.

There are many factors to be considered in determining if a symbol user should be encouraged to express in symbols all the words that occur in a spoken or written English sentence or if the user should be allowed to leave out function words and other words not essential to meaning (*Handbook of Blissymbolics*, pp.43—46). Evaluation of the two factors discussed below sometimes produces indications that the symbol user should be encouraged to use the simplest type of language structure.

Physical capability. Many children who cannot speak intelligibly also have poor control of their arms and hands; hence; pointing to symbols is laborious and imprecise. It is often advisable to encourage these children to use only those words needed to transmit their message. Insistence on following a mature language model may cause communication to progress so slowly that inter-personal relationships are discouraged. Also, for the imprecise pointer, it is frequently necessary to limit the number of symbols displayed. In this case only highly functional words/symbols can be included in the display.

Level of cognitive functioning. Some symbol users are unable to generate or understand long sequences of words. Rather than demand that they communicate in grammatically correct sentences, they might be encouraged to express their feelings, thoughts, needs and questions using single word/symbols or with short combinations of words.

In Chapter VIII types of symbol instruction will be discussed. Further consideration will be given to the question of what type of syntax the child should be taught and expected to use.

V. How to Draw Blissymbols

To persons accustomed to reading their language it is obvious that the letters that make up words may be formed in many different ways without affecting legibility or meaning. A variety of type faces is available to the printer, such as Roman, Italic, bold face and light face. The appearance of a letter differs with the type face. Further, different sizes of the same letter (capital and small) may be used yet the meaning remains clear. Handwriting is a highly individualistic skill and the script produced ranges from illegible to artistic. The shape of a given letter as written by different persons varies widely. Many writers make no effort to keep the size of one letter proportional to the others or to maintain a uniform vertical or horizontal positioning of letters, yet someone familiar with the written form of the language can read and understand what was written. In the written forms of languages such as English and French only the approximate shape of a letter carries information. For these languages, such characteristics as size and position in relation to a base line are not significant.

One might assume that similar freedom of artistic expression and individualism might be allowed in drawing Blissymbols; however, as explained earlier, the meaning of a symbol is determined by its *configuration* or shape, *size* in relation to the dimensions of the square, which has been chosen as the frame of reference, *position* or location within the frame of reference, *direction* of symbol parts and *spacing* between parts of certain symbols. Clearly the writing of messages in Blissymbols requires a degree of precision and attention to detail not required in writing messages in English or French. A sloppily located $+$ might have the reader wondering if the writer meant *belongs to, and*, or *with the help of*. Placement of the pointer $\vee$ cannot be approached as casually as dotting an ''i'' or crossing a ''t'', nor can the writer draw a circle as freely as writing the letter ''o''. A capital ''O'' and a small letter ''o'' would have the same significance. A large circle $\bigcirc$ would mean *sun* but a small circle centered on the midline of the frame of reference $\circ$ would mean *mouth*. Careless drawing of $\cap$ or $\wedge$ might result in confusion between *knowledge* $\sqcap$ and *house* $\triangle$.

Blissymbols may be drawn under several circumstances. In preparing material for publication such as a book, journal article, newspaper story or a newsletter to be disseminated to other than a local program, symbols should be drawn with precision and to the specifications set down by the Blissymbolics Communication Institution. For such publications, symbols should be submitted to BCI for approval while the publication is in manuscript form and the publication must note that the symbols used are covered by copyright. The intent of such review is to maintain the standard symbol form essential to a universal meaning. When preparing materials for bulletin boards, communication boards, or classroom activities, the use of graph paper or a template is recommended in order to produce accurate symbols. When drawing symbols to represent a message formulated by a symbol user or when writing a message in symbols, drawing with a template or graph paper would be tediously slow and would destroy the spontaneity of communication. For such purposes freehand drawing of symbols is advised; however, the person drawing symbols should be careful to observe those symbol features which are important for indicating meaning and which distinguish one symbol from another, such as shape, size, direction, etc.

The square

All symbols used in representing the words of a message must be scaled in size, positioned, and directionally oriented with reference to the *same* square.

Below are three squares. The first is 1 inch, the second 20 millimeters and the third is 10 millimeters.

Reading across you will note that even though the symbols become smaller they have the same meaning. Reading down you will note that a symbol of the same shape but of a different size has a different meaning; hence,

1. meaning changes if size of frame of reference remains constant but size of symbol changes.
2. meaning does not change if symbol size changes in proportion to frame of reference.

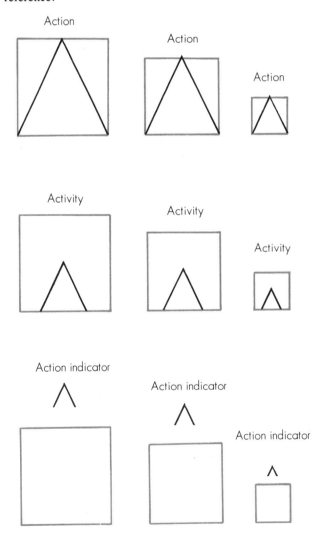

Location is determined in relation to the earthline, midline (horizontal and vertical) and skyline. The same symbol has different meanings depending on its location within the frame of reference as, illustrated below:

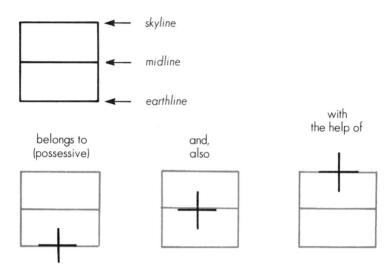

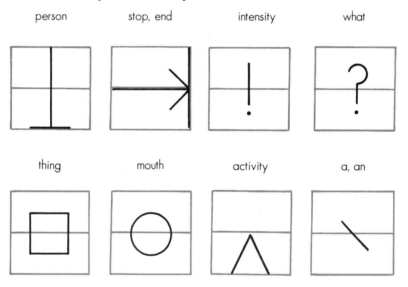

The vertical and horizontal midlines serve as guides for locating the elements of certain symbols if the symbol is drawn alone.

In the vertical dimension the position of a symbol in relation to earthline and skyline remains constant. The position of a symbol in the horizontal dimension will be discussed later in connection with the rules for drawing compound symbols and symbol sentences.

Templates

Plastic forms are available in three sizes. Each contains shapes that can be used as patterns for copying symbol elements. The sizes are shown below:

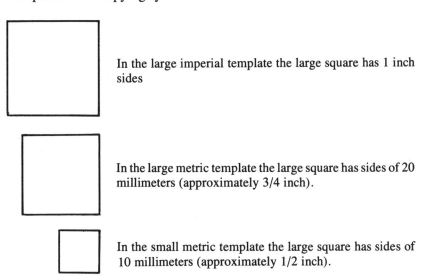

In the large imperial template the large square has 1 inch sides

In the large metric template the large square has sides of 20 millimeters (approximately 3/4 inch).

In the small metric template the large square has sides of 10 millimeters (approximately 1/2 inch).

The small metric template is illustrated below, for space reasons. However, the symbols in the drawing section are drawn to the scale of the larger metric template, for clarity of shapes and angles.

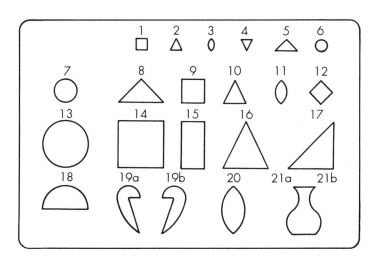

Observe that when the square (number 14) is used as the frame of reference for drawing symbols, shapes 13 and 21 are full size. Shapes 7 through 12 are half size and shapes 1 through 6 are quarter size. This arrangement provides the necessary patterns for drawing symbols or symbol elements to their appropriate scale: full, half or quarter. Note that the triangles numbered 16, 10 and 2 have acute angles. This angle is used in drawing the symbols for *man, woman* and *to walk*. The angle is used also in drawing the description (evaluation) indicator, the action indicator and the active and passive indicators. Symbol components such as the arrow head, pointer and protection symbol are drawn with the 90 degree angle. Care must be exercised to avoid interchanging these angles when drawing symbols.

Notice also that the arc of the curve in the full-size figure 20 is not the same as the arc in 13 or 18. Note the difference in the following symbols for *body* and for *knowledge*:

body

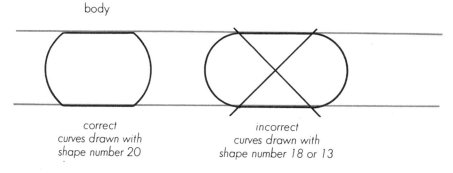

correct
curves drawn with
shape number 20

incorrect
curves drawn with
shape number 18 or 13

Similarly the arcs in the half-size shapes number 11 and 7 are unlike, as are the arcs in the quarter size shapes 3 and 6. As with the different angles, the symbol drawer should be careful not to use the incorrect arc in drawing a symbol or symbol element.

knowledge

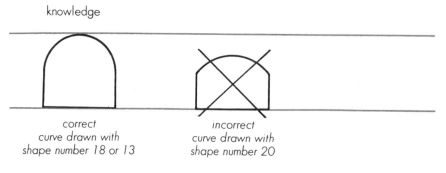

correct
curve drawn with
shape number 18 or 13

incorrect
curve drawn with
shape number 20

The symbol drawing error most likely to occur when using the template results from selecting the incorrect size of a shape. Following are some examples of correct use of the forms appearing on the templates.

1. *Triangles with acute angles (16, 10, 2 and 4)*

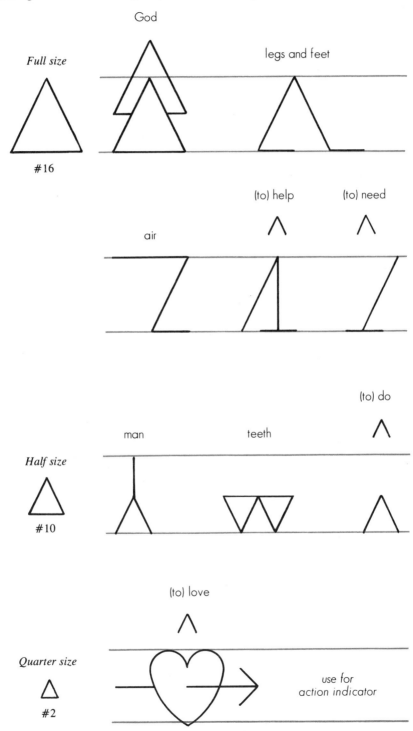

God

Full size

legs and feet

#16

(to) help   (to) need

air

(to) do

man   teeth

Half size

#10

(to) love

Quarter size

#2

use for
action indicator

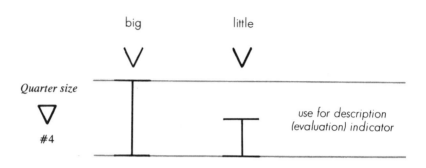

2. *Right-angled triangles (17, 8, 5)* (Note 90 degree angle)

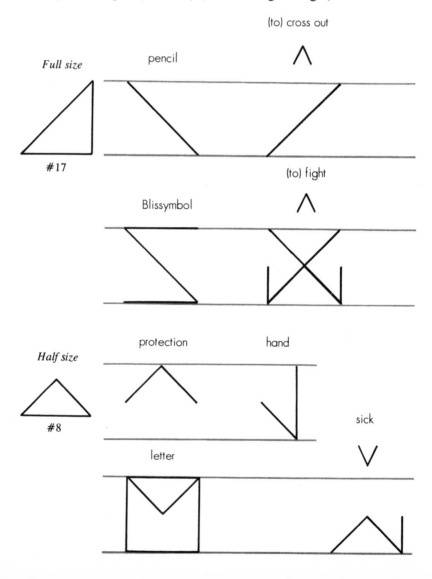

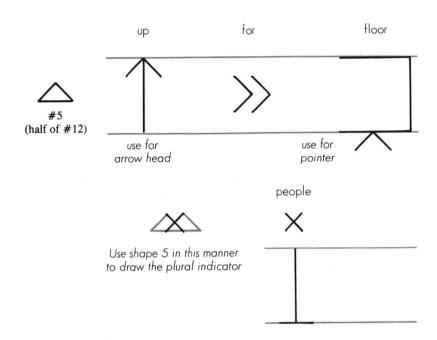

#5
(half of #12)

up

use for
arrow head

for

floor

use for
pointer

Use shape 5 in this manner
to draw the plural indicator

people

3. Squares (14, 9, 1)

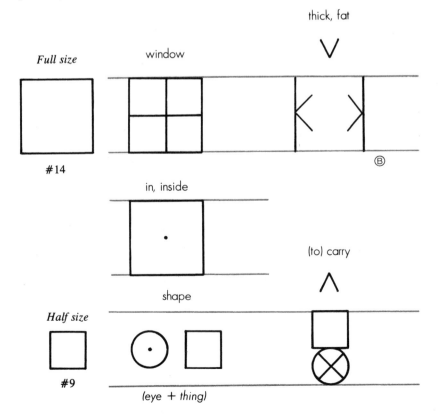

Full size

window

thick, fat

#14

in, inside

ⓑ

(to) carry

shape

Half size

#9

(eye + thing)

Also used to draw diagonal lines as below:

a, an   that

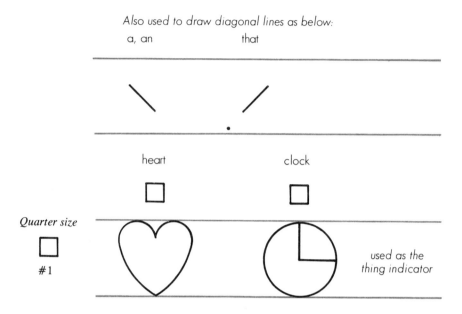

heart   clock

Quarter size   *used as the thing indicator*

#1

4. Circles (13, 7, 6 and the semi-circle 18)

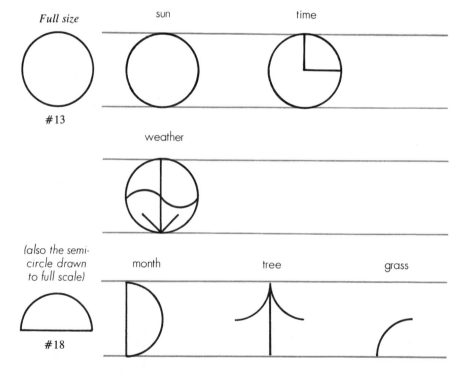

Full size   sun   time

#13

weather

(also the semi-circle drawn to full scale)   month   tree   grass

#18

fish

mouth   needle   maybe

Half size

⭕

#7

library

Quarter size

⭕

#6

used in the
combine
indicator

used in drawing the top portion
of the question mark

5. Leaf shape (20, 11, 3)

(to) keep, save

present

Full size

#20

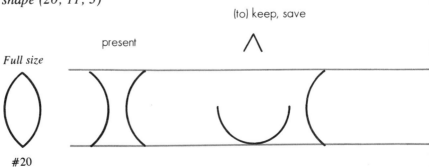

leaf

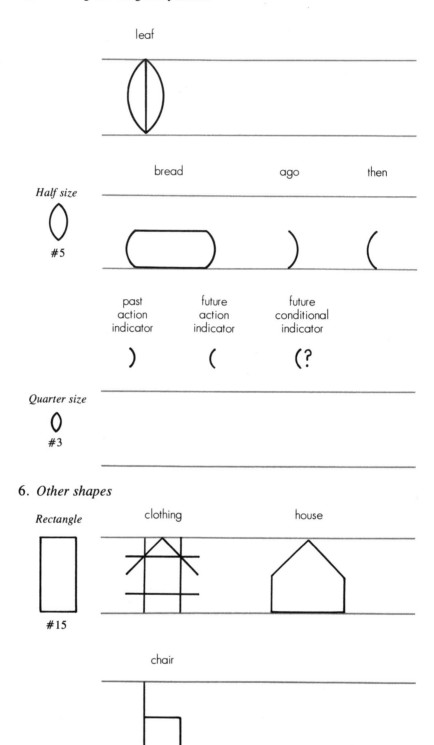

bread   ago   then

Half size

#5

past   future   future
action   action   conditional
indicator   indicator   indicator

)   ((?

Quarter size

#3

6. Other shapes

Rectangle   clothing   house

#15

chair

Diamond

Note that shape number 12 is actually a square but smaller than the half-size square.

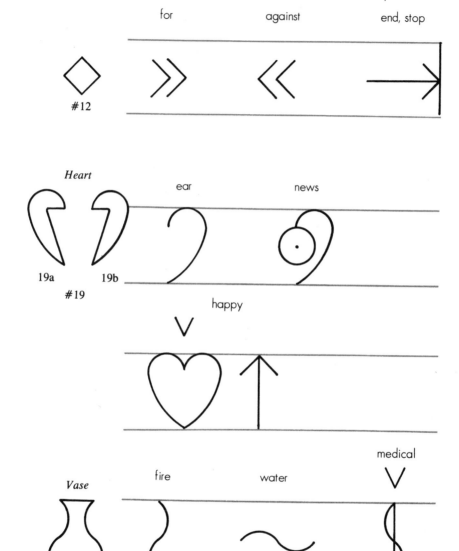

The Blissymbolics Communication Institute has developed specifications as indicated for drawing the following symbols:

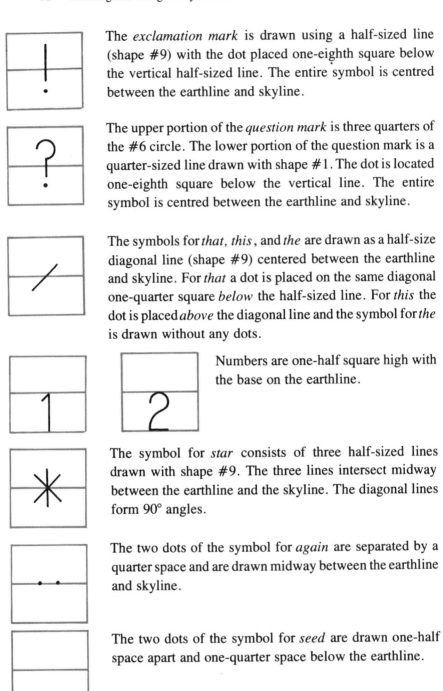

The *exclamation mark* is drawn using a half-sized line (shape #9) with the dot placed one-eighth square below the vertical half-sized line. The entire symbol is centred between the earthline and skyline.

The upper portion of the *question mark* is three quarters of the #6 circle. The lower portion of the question mark is a quarter-sized line drawn with shape #1. The dot is located one-eighth square below the vertical line. The entire symbol is centred between the earthline and skyline.

The symbols for *that, this*, and *the* are drawn as a half-size diagonal line (shape #9) centered between the earthline and skyline. For *that* a dot is placed on the same diagonal one-quarter square *below* the half-sized line. For *this* the dot is placed *above* the diagonal line and the symbol for *the* is drawn without any dots.

Numbers are one-half square high with the base on the earthline.

The symbol for *star* consists of three half-sized lines drawn with shape #9. The three lines intersect midway between the earthline and the skyline. The diagonal lines form 90° angles.

The two dots of the symbol for *again* are separated by a quarter space and are drawn midway between the earthline and skyline.

The two dots of the symbol for *seed* are drawn one-half space apart and one-quarter space below the earthline.

Drawing the indicators

Indicators are drawn with the appropriate *one-quarter size* shapes and when used with a single symbol are drawn one-quarter space above the horizontal center of the symbol.

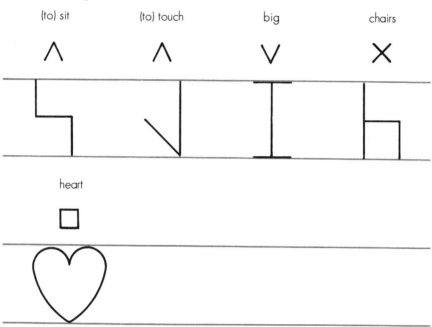

When drawing compound or combined symbols the indicator is drawn one-quarter space above the horizontal center *of the classifier*. In the examples below the classifier is the first symbol.

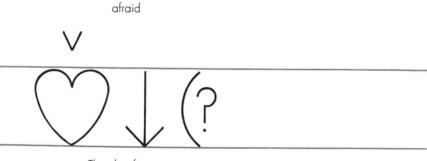

(to) learn

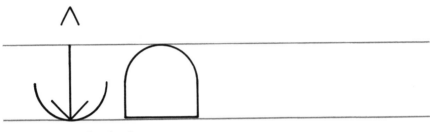

The classifier is
(to) receive

friends

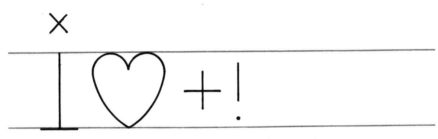

The classifier is
person

Sometimes, as in the symbols for *angry, dirty, early,* and *quiet,* the classifier is not the first symbol in the sequence, nevertheless, *the indicator is drawn above the classifier* rather than above the first symbol in the sequence.

angry

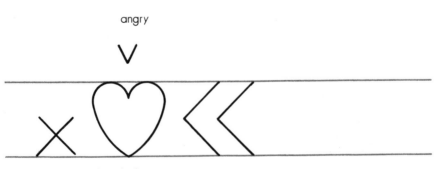

much + feeling + opposition
The classifier is feeling

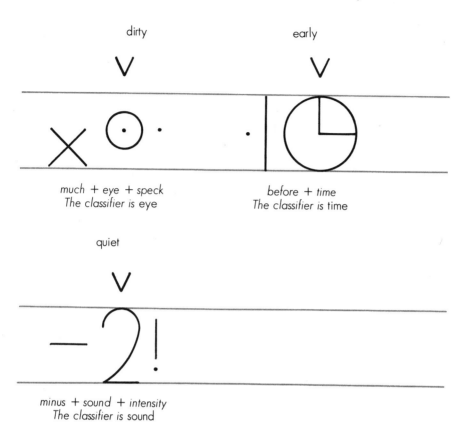

dirty

early

much + eye + speck
The classifier is eye

before + time
The classifier is time

quiet

minus + sound + intensity
The classifier is sound

Similarly the indicator does not appear over the symbol for *opposite meaning, more,* or *most* when it is the first symbol in the sequence. In sequential compounds using as indicator, the indicator is placed over *the classifier.*

stupid

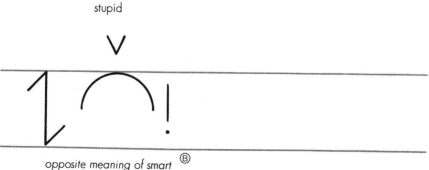

opposite meaning of smart   Ⓑ
The classifier is mind

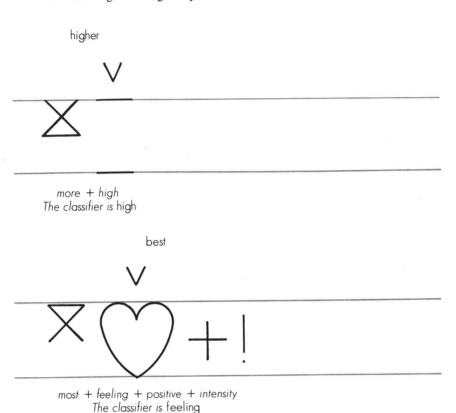

higher

more + high
The classifier is high

best

most + feeling + positive + intensity
The classifier is feeling

The combine indicator

Symbols sequenced by a symbol user or an instructor to express a meaning
for which an approved symbol is not available comprise a combined symbol.
Such symbols are preceded and followed by *combine indicators* which are
drawn one-quarter space above the skyline. One-quarter space separates the
first combine indicator from the first symbol and a similar space separates
the last symbol and the second combine indicator.

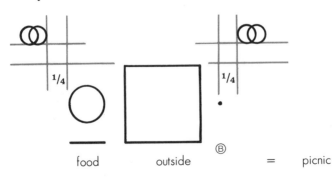

food   outside   =   picnic

Spacing between symbols

1. Symbols in a sequential compound

Within a sequential compound *one-quarter space* separates the individual components. This separation is measured from the extreme right of the first symbol (or the one to the left if there are more than two symbols in the compound) to the extreme left of the following symbol.

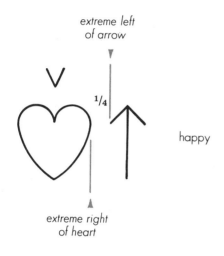

extreme left
of arrow

$^1/_4$

extreme right
of heart

happy

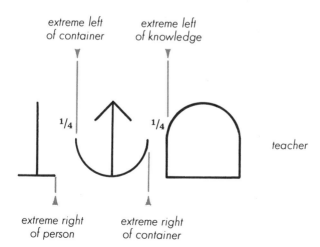

extreme left
of container

extreme left
of knowledge

$^1/_4$ $^1/_4$

teacher

extreme right
of person

extreme right
of container

2. Symbols in a sentence

A full space beginning at the furthest extension of the preceding symbol separates independent symbols in a sentence. A sequential compound is treated as a single unit or an independent symbol. The quarter spacing between symbols making up the compound is observed when a sequential compound appears in a sentence.

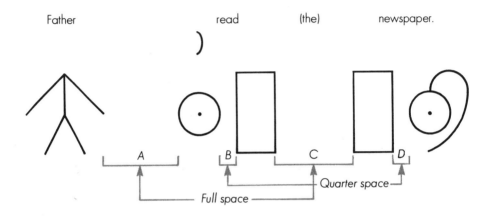

A. *Full space* between independent symbols *father* and *read*.

B. *Quarter space* between symbols for *eye* (*with action indicator in the past*) and *page* — which make up the sequential compound *read*.

C. *Full space* between independent symbols *read* and *newspaper*.

D. *Quarter space* between symbols for *paper*, *page* and *news* (*eye + ear*).

VI. Developing a Blissymbolics Training Program

Preparation for symbol instruction

Before beginning to teach Blissymbolics to a child — or to a group of children — it is essential to explain Blissymbolics to the persons with whom the symbol users will interact and to enlist their cooperation. The symbol instructor must constantly bear in mind that communication involves an active relationship between the expressing person and the receiving person. It will do no good to train a child in the use of symbols if there are no opportunities to use the symbols in communication. Further, it is essential that the Blissymbolics program not be a pet project of the symbol instructor. Projects started in this manner will not be optimally effective for handicapped persons and may even fail. The Blissymbolics program should be organized as a project of the school, hospital or other setting in which it is offered. Through conferences and in-service training programs, key persons in the child's community must be provided with information about:

1. why development of a non-speech expressive modality is necessary;
2. the nature of Blissymbols and the symbol system;
3. how they (the key persons) can facilitate communication with the symbol user.

1. Administrators

Before initiating a symbol training program, the symbol instructor should explain Blissymbolics, the nature of initial and on-going assessment and the training program to appropriate members of the administrative staff. It is advisable to obtain administrative approval of the Blissymbolics program before contacting parents, conducting in-service programs for staff or initiating symbol training with children. It is particularly important to have the support of those persons charged with supervision of the child's educational programs. As noted earlier, some professional workers are strongly opposed to the teaching of non-speech communication. When an administrator or supervisor feels that communication systems such as Blissymbolics are detrimental or of little value it is not likely that the support and cooperation needed for developing a successful Blissymbolic communication program will be forthcoming. Rarely, if ever, can a symbol instructor's enthusiasm offset the negative attitudes of administrators or supervisors.

It is important to have publicity for a Blissymbolics program. Through stories in newspapers, and radio and television programs, the public can be informed about communication problems and the importance of providing non-speaking children with a way of expressing themselves. In this way a climate of acceptance can be created, making it easier for the symbol user to become a member of the community. The symbol instructor should work within appropriate administrative channels in developing a public information program and when responding to requests for stories about Blissymbolics. It is essential that the Blissymbolics program be viewed not as a special activity of the symbol instructor but as a special program of the school or institution.

2. Parents

Many parents resist the teaching and use of any non-speech method of communication. They naturally want their child to be as "normal" as possible. One of the first things normally developing children learn is how to talk. It has often been noted that the ability to speak is uniquely human; hence, not to speak represents a failure to develop an important human characteristic. It is not unusual for parents to insist that they can understand everything the child says, and it is true that considerable information can be transmitted from child to parent via the oral-audio route even when the child can produce only a few differentiated vocalizations. However, analysis of how the communication occurs reveals that the parents rely on questioning, guessing, context clues and intuition to interpret the vocalizations.

Through conferences and discussions parents can be helped to understand the importance of being able to express oneself in a modality that can be readily interpreted by persons who do not know the child well enough to understand idiosyncratic communication efforts. The child should be able to communicate in a wide variety of settings, not just within the close family group. Parents need to realize that when speech is difficult to understand, communication suffers and their child is cut off from opportunities to learn and develop through social interactions. It should be stressed that the use of speech will be continued even though expression using symbols is being emphasized. It might be demonstrated that the child's simultaneous pointing to a symbol and vocalizing will make the speech more meaningful to a listener.

The instructor should be prepared to show parents symbols for a basic vocabulary and to explain how meanings of symbols are changed and how symbols are sequenced to make simple sentences. Some parents may want a deeper explanation of the symbol system. When possible the instructor should arrange for parents to observe children communicating with symbols and to talk with other parents. If a live demonstration of symbol use is not possible, a showing of videotapes might be scheduled for parents.

The parents' advice should be solicited in selecting the first symbols to be taught and, as the symbol program progresses, parents should be kept informed about new symbols or new parts of the symbol system the child is learning. It is important to ask parents what symbols they think the child needs. Suggestions for providing the child with opportunities for symbol use at home should be made regularly.

3. Professional workers

There are many reasons why speech/language pathologists, teachers and other professional workers may be reluctant to teach children to express themselves by some means other than speech. Until recently, training in speech pathology focused on teaching the speech-handicapped how to talk and little attention was given to language or communication. The decision to teach non-speech expression represented a failure to carry out the professional's speech-teaching mission. Further, it was assumed that allowing the child to communicate by gesture or other non-speech mode of expression would interfere with speech development. As a result, children were often enrolled in speech training programs long past the time when all evidence indicated a poor prognosis for developing intelligible speech.

This view is no longer tenable. For some time professional workers have cited instances in which children actually became more vocal and their speech more intelligible after they began using a non-speech mode of communication. In addition to such anecdotal indications that the proper teaching of a non-speech mode of communication does not interfere with but may facilitate development of intelligible speech is the finding of the BCI Evaluation Study: ''Where oral communication is no longer the central focus of attention, spontaneous changes seem to occur with increased clarity of speech'' (*Handbook of Blissymbolics*, Evaluation Study, p.82).

Teachers are trained to teach children to read words and sentences printed in a traditional alphabet. Since this is the form in which newspapers, books and other reading material are printed, it is often argued that children must learn the conventional symbols. To teach a child any other symbol system may mean that the teacher is not fulfilling the requirements of a standard curriculum. Again, it is argued that use of another symbol system will interfere with learning to read words and sentences constructed of conventional letters arranged according to accepted orthography. This concern is probably unwarranted. While the effect learning Blissymbols has on learning to read words has not been thoroughly studied, clinical experience suggests that training in the use of Blissymbols prepares ''for reading through experience with the process but not directly with the content of the written English system'' (*Handbook of Blissymbolics*, Appendix 10, p.414). Changes in reading level of children in the Evaluation Study suggested ''that symbol instruction does not negatively affect reading performance even in the short term'' (*Handbook of Blissymbolics*, Evaluation Study, p.77).

In-service training programs should explain that some children will not be able to develop intelligible speech regardless of how much training they receive. Other children demonstrate marked difficulty in learning to extract meaning from conventional visual displays of words and sentences. Some of these children may be able to learn how to use Blissymbolics. An introduction to Blissymbolics should be presented to professional workers so they can become familiar with the appearance and interpretation of symbols and how the system can provide for language structures that correspond to those used in conventional speaking, reading and writing.

Where possible, other professional workers in addition to the symbol instructor should be involved in selecting children for the symbol program. Their involvement should include review and discussion of the assessment data. After a child is enrolled in the symbol training program, professional persons who work with the child should be encouraged to suggest symbols to be taught. Once the symbol program is initiated, the symbol instructor must continue to work closely with the other professional workers to keep them up to date about those aspects of Blissymbolics the child has learned. Working together, the symbol instructor and other professional workers should structure situations, design assignments and other tasks to bring the symbol-user into the group and provide opportunities for communication.

4. Care providers

In some situations there are persons other than the parents who attend to the child's needs. They might be called surrogate parents, foster grandparents, attendants, aides, cottage personnel or some other name. They spend much time with the child and engage in activities where communication would naturally take place. Just as the routine activities of bathing, feeding, toileting, dressing, etc. provide opportunities for communication between parent and child, these on-going events provide a natural setting for communication between child and caretaker. Children who cannot speak intelligibly are likely to be passive recipients of care. Communicative interactions which are vital to the child's development never take place.

Some care providers will resist suggestions that they should encourage the child to communicate about feelings, ask questions and be given opportunities to make simple choices and decisions. They may argue that there isn't enough time. Other care providers may indicate a sincere interest in communicating with the children but feel that they don't know how. This is especially true in the case of those children whose speech is unintelligible.

Care providers are so important in the child's life that the symbol instructor should make every effort to arouse their interest in the symbol program. Working with the symbol instructor, care providers might find ways of incorporating symbol communication into their activities by changing their approach without having to spend more time with a child. For example, during feeding the child might be encouraged to use symbols to indicate what food is wanted next —a drink of milk, a spoonful of potatoes, or a bite of meat. At playtime care providers can encourage children to use their symbols to indicate what toy or game is wanted. At bedtime symbols might be used to indicate if the child prefers to be bathed first or have teeth brushed first. Care providers can learn to be on the lookout for ways in which the child can use symbols to have some influence on what happens to him or her. It would be advantageous to all the children if care providers could accept the view that *communicating with* is as important as *administering to* a child.

In-service training of child care personnel prior to initiating a symbol training program is highly important. The in-service training program must contain provision for getting feed-back from care providers, expanding their knowledge of Blissymbolics and communication techniques, and for training new members of the care-provider staff. Communication training programs in some institutions have failed because they were not supported by the care provider personnel. In other situations symbol training programs have been successfully established partly because of the interest and support of the care providers (Harris, et al, "Symbol Communication for the Mentally Retarded," *Mental Retardation*, 13:1, 1975).

5. Siblings and peers

It has been emphasized that communication takes place within a community. Brothers, sisters, classmates and friends make up an important part of the symbol user's community. Frequent communication between symbol users and persons in this group will occur naturally if peers and siblings learn about Blissymbolics and how to relate to a symbol user. Even though other people can interpret a symbol message by reading the words printed above the symbols, interest in interacting with the symbol user will be heightened if siblings and peers understand the symbols and symbol system. When a child responds in symbols in the classroom the teacher might use the occasion to explain to the other pupils the nature and meaning of the symbols used. Many children's table games that use words and pictures can be adapted for play using symbols. In the *Handbook of Blissymbolics*, instructions are given for constructing many toys, games and teaching aids (Appendices 5 and 6, pp.310, 346). Periodically, similar materials and activities are described in the *Newsletter*.

If siblings and friends are given a copy of the symbols a handicapped child is learning in a residential center they can send letters by copying appropriate symbols. This should be encouraged even if some symbols are incorrectly drawn or the syntax incorrect, because of the value of the social interaction. The symbol instructor can use the letters for lessons in symbol drawing or syntax.

These preliminary steps may seem unnecessary. The symbol instructor quite naturally is eager to begin teaching children to use Blissymbols. The natural tendency is to jump immediately into an assessment and instructional program and postpone or overlook making the essential preparations for the program. This can prove to be disastrous! Unless the symbol program has the support of parents, administrators and staff personnel at all levels the program will fail or only partially meet its objectives: to enable non-speaking children to express their ideas and feelings to and to ask questions of members of their community.

VII. Assessment

It has become a standard procedure for psychologists, teachers and therapists to test children in order to determine their readiness for certain learning tasks or to predict how well they will develop skills or acquire knowledge. Batteries of tests are often administered in the hope that learning problems may be identified and circumvented. (See *Handbook of Blissymbolics*, pp.131–139, for a description of formal assessment devices.) The value of using tests with children whose communication skills are severely limited is questionable. Certainly professional workers should be cautious about using test results as a basis for determining a child's readiness to learn Blissymbols or for predicting how well a child can learn to communicate with Blissymbols. With children who cannot speak intelligibly or produce messages graphically, carefully planned and conducted diagnostic teaching is often a more effective way of determining what they can learn.

Questions to be answered
1. How does the child attempt to communicate?
2. About what does the child attempt to communicate?
3. With whom does the child attempt to communicate?
4. How does the child react when attempts to communicate are unsuccessful?
5. What are the characteristics of the child's cognitive-perceptual functioning?

An inventory of the child's methods of revealing a feeling, signalling a need or communicating a thought will aid the instructor in detecting responses which might easily be overlooked. Such an inventory may be compiled through discussions with parents and others who are familiar with the child and by careful observation of the child when tasks requiring responses are presented. It is essential to bear in mind that non-speaking children whose severe physical handicaps limit use of arms and hands often develop gestures consisting of minimal movement of some part of the body. They have no way of indicating with what part of the body the movement will be made or what it means. They can only hope that an observer will be sufficiently interested to search for it and, when detected, sufficiently concerned to work at determining the child's intended meaning. Many people — including some who have professional training — are so accustomed to communicating through speech that attempts to communicate in another mode are overlooked.

1. How does the child attempt to communicate?

When making an inventory of a child's methods of communicating it is also essential to keep in mind that it is possible to communicate via signals, signs, and idiosyncratic symbols as well as by conventional symbols.

Signals. In this discussion of how non-speaking children communicate we use the term *signal* to mean an action on the part of the child which triggers a response in another person. A child in the pre-language stage uses cries of various types as signals to indicate hunger, pain, fatigue and excretory activity. Other types of vocalization are used to indicate comfort and pleasure. The alert observer will note that, as the infant grows older, different types of body activity are associated with the various body states. In the infant the sounds and movements are involuntary and, in the normally developing child, they are gradually replaced by speech and gestures. Many children who have difficulty developing intelligible speech retain the early sounds and movements and produce them voluntarily in attempts to transmit messages. The voluntary use of even these primitive signals to transmit a message suggests that the non-speaking child has discovered the social utility of communication. When a child demonstrates awareness that the performance of certain acts (sound making or body movement) will result in desirable responses from other people, the teaching of a higher level of communication system should be considered.

Signs. In this discussion we use the term *sign* to refer to a movement, or movements, of a part, or parts, of the body to transmit a message. Verbal mediation is involved in the development of these movements in contrast to the "signal" movements which evolve from earlier reflex activities. Signs have been used to communicate by many groups, such as the American Indians and the deaf. The literature on manual communication systems is extensive. For this discussion of assessment, our interest is not in the advanced use of signing as a communication mode, but rather in the possible significance of gestures that are self-developed or incidentally learned by young non-speaking children. One child conveyed that she was thinking about Santa Claus by moving her hand downward with the first and second fingers separated and extended. After much guessing her parents hit on the thought that the gesture represented Santa's legs as he came down the chimney and the delighted child nodded affirmation. Another child based many gestures on the children's stories and nursery rhymes read to her by her parents. The days of the week were indicated by a vertical movement of fist and hand for Monday and a horizontal movement for Tuesday from the rhyme "This is the way we wash our clothes early Monday morning. This is the way we iron our clothes early Tuesday morning . . . ." The use of such signs or gestures indicates that the child understands language and can express it in some modality other than speech. Children with these capabilities may be good candidates for symbol training. Actually, symbol formulation and expression are involved in their use of signs to transmit messages.

Symbols. A symbol is not the "real" thing. A symbol represents something. Communication usually involves the use of symbols that have conventional meanings. Information transfer occurs when the observer or listener interprets the symbol as the symbol producer intended. The communicative value of a symbol increases as more members of the community produce and interpret the symbol in the same way. The symbols some children produce differ from those produced by other members of their community; hence they have reduced communicative value. The child may have thoughts which would be understood by the community but, because of a problem with language expression or speech production, the symbols are peculiar to the speaker. To stress that these symbols mean something to the child, if not to the community, we suggest the term *idiosyncratic symbols*. Generally, understanding improves as one becomes more familiar with the child's idiosyncratic symbols; however, adequate communication is usually possible with only one or two people. The fact that the child uses symbols suggests that learning a different symbol system might be possible.

When exploring the question of how the child attempts to communicate, two aspects of message transmission are to be noted: first, the nature of the overt behavior by which the message is transmitted (for example, vocalization, body movement) and, second, the form of the message (for example, signal, sign, idiosyncratic symbols, conventional symbols).

An effective method of obtaining information about a child's communication skills is to ask questions which cannot be answered "yes" or "no" but which instead elicit a description of the child's behavior. The following questions illustrate this approach:

1. What kinds of things does CN (child's name) tell you?
   Here we would look for examples of expression of needs, feelings, ideas. These examples often suggest what symbols might be immediately useful to the child.
2. How does CN tell you . . . ?
   Here we would ask about many of the examples given in response to

the first question. Again, it is important to obtain specific descriptions of the child's method of expression, because this information will facilitate communication with the child during early symbol training.

a. Vocalization

If the informant indicates that the child communicates by making sounds, clarify the nature of the vocalizations. Determine if the informant identifies the vocalizations as words used by the child and check how easily the words can be understood, using categories such as those suggested below:

(i)   can be understood by anyone without difficulty;

(ii) can be understood readily by persons accustomed to child's speech;

(iii) meaning usually can be determined using context clues and some guessing;

(iv) even persons accustomed to child's speech have difficulty understanding unless they know in general what child is talking about.

Symbols might be taught early to express words that the child tries to say but cannot express immediately.

If the child's vocalizations are not intelligible as words, determine the nature of the vocalizations and when they are used. Ask the informant, "What messages does CN get across to you by making sounds?" Obtaining a complete list of the messages transmitted by this method not only provides clues as to what symbols to teach but also gives some information about the child's understanding of the social utility of language. Obtain from the informant also a description of the different vocalizations produced by CN, noting particularly how the vocalizations differ from each other.

b. Pointing or gesturing

It is important to distinguish between pointing and gesturing and to obtain descriptions of how the child uses each. *Pointing*, as used here, refers to aiming some part of the body (for example, finger, head, eye) in the direction of an object that the child wants to indicate. *Gesturing*, as used here, refers to moving a part, or parts, of the body to express the child's intent. Pointing skill is an asset in using a communication board. Accurate pointing enables a child to indicate directly the symbol selected for a message. The more labored and the less accurate the child's pointing, the more difficult it will be to indicate for an observer which of the displayed symbols the child wants to incorporate into a message. It is important to note how the child points, that is, which part of the body is aimed toward the object or symbol. With this information, symbol displays can be arranged to allow the child to use the movements which are best controlled. (See *Handbook of Blissymbolics*, pp.63–85 for a discussion of testing pointing ability and techniques of positioning and handtraining toward symbol use, and pp.418–448 for a step-by-step description of how to develop "eye-pointing.")

Gesturing is more complex than pointing both in the linguistic characteristics of the message and in the nature of the motor act. Knowledge of the child's gestural repertoire will aid in selecting items and developing methods for symbol training.

2. About what does the child attempt to communicate?

What a child tries to communicate would be influenced by the nature of his cognitive development. It is not our purpose here to explore this relationship. Our interest in the question is two-fold. First, we assume that the greater the number of topics about which a child tries to communicate, the greater will be his interest in learning Blissymbols. Second, a list of the kinds of things a child "talks" about will provide guidance in selecting symbols to be taught.

3. With whom does the child attempt to communicate?

The significance of this question is three-fold. Children who interact with many people may have a stronger desire to acquire communication skills than the child who attempts to communicate only with mother. Psycho-social growth is reflected in a widening scope of interpersonal relations and communication plays an important part in initiating and maintaining these relations. Secondly, the persons with whom a child attempts to communicate may suggest vocabulary items for which symbols are needed and they can provide real-life opportunities for practice in communicating with symbols. Thirdly, it will be necessary to teach those persons with whom the child tries to communicate about symbols and how the child uses them.

4. How does the child react when attempts to communicate are unsuccessful?

Reactions are varied. Some children quickly give up. Others persist in trying to "get across" what they have in mind but continue to act in a stereotyped way, others exhibit flexibility and try different ways to transmit their message. Some remain placid — even passive — while others become frustrated. Children who persist and who make divergent efforts to express their feelings and thoughts are more likely to perceive how another symbol system might facilitate communication than are those who make little effort to communicate.

5. What are the characteristics of the child's cognitive-perceptual functioning?

Determining the level of intellectual development of a child whose expressive capabilities are severely limited is difficult. Sometimes the only way to determine if a child can learn to communicate by pointing to pictures or symbols is through a trial of teaching. Clearly, though, it would be useless to attempt to teach symbols to a child who is functioning at a pre-symbolic level. Normally developing children are thought to begin dissociation of external actions and mental representations at about eighteen to twenty-four months. At that time they begin to learn how to represent objects and actions internally. They can use a word or an image to stand for something. From then on their symbolic system develops rapidly. Initially the child's symbols are idiosyncratic but, as the language of the community is learned, the child's symbol formulation follows the patterns of the community.

Between two and three years of age, children whose cognitive and perceptual development is progressing normally demonstrate ability to classify or group real objects, small likenesses of real objects, and pictures. Of possible significance for the teaching of symbols is the observation that children of this age have difficulty grouping or classifying abstract forms such as circles, squares and triangles. Development of a capacity for symbolic representation and the ability to recognize and group or classify abstract forms is markedly delayed in some children; however, the possibility should be considered that even though a child has not learned to classify *abstract* forms he might be able to classify the meaning-referenced shapes of Bliss pictographs.

Children whose failure to develop intelligible speech is associated with severe mental retardation (I.Q. 20–30) may not develop the cognitive abilities prerequisite for symbol learning until six years of age or older. Profoundly retarded persons (I.Q. less than 20) will develop a capacity for symbolic representation much later and some may never internalize their sensorimotor behavior patterns and develop symbolic representations. Some children with a normal rate of cognitive-perceptual development cannot develop intelligible speech because of neuromuscular dysfunction. They should begin demonstrating cognitive-perceptual prerequisites for symbol learning when about three years of age.

Assessment Inventory

As instructors gain experience in teaching symbols they usually like to develop their own assessment procedures and record forms. Assessment procedures and forms developed by the Blissymbolics Communication Institute are described and the prognostic value of various pre-training assessments discussed in the *Handbook of Blissymbolics*, pp.93–130. The inventory which follows is designed to gather information pertinent to the assessment questions posed on pp.96-100.

FACTORS TO BE CONSIDERED IN DEVELOPING A COMMUNICATION TRAINING PROGRAM (CHECK *YES, NO,* OR APPROPRIATE ITEMS AND GIVE EXAMPLES WHERE INDICATED)

	YES	NO
I. Present method of communication		
A. Interest in communicating	☐	☐
1. Seems to make no attempt to communicate	☐	☐
2. Tries to communicate but gives up if not quickly understood	☐	☐
3. Persists but uses stereotyped efforts to make self understood	☐	☐
4. Persists using varied approaches to make self understood	☐	☐
B. Uses speech to communicate	☐	☐

      1. Estimated number of words in vocabulary_____

      2. Speech consists of (check one)

          ☐ single-word utterances

          ☐ two-word utterances

          ☐ utterances of three or more words

      3. Intelligibility (check one)

          ☐ can be understood by anyone without difficulty

☐ can be understood readily by persons accustomed to child's speech

☐ meaning usually can be determined using context clues and some guessing

☐ even persons accustomed to child's speech have difficulty understanding unless they know in general what child is talking about

☐ utterances are usually unintelligible

4. On the back of this sheet list the child's expressive vocabulary and give examples of multiple word utterances.

                                                              YES   NO
C. Uses vocalizations other than speech to communicate   ☐   ☐

   ☐ cries
   ☐ vowel-like sounds
   other noises (describe) _____

   _____

   _____

D. Uses gestures to communicate   ☐   ☐
   ☐ wanting
   ☐ rejecting
   Other — Describe fully enough that an observer
   would recognize it _____

   _____

   _____

   _____

   _____

   _____

   _____

E. Uses pointing to communicate   ☐   ☐
   1. Arm and hand   ☐   ☐

      ☐ points with one finger
         ☐ right hand   ☐ left hand

points with fingers but can't isolate only one finger

☐ right hand   ☐ left hand

points grossly with a fisted hand

☐ right hand   ☐ left hand

                                                YES   NO

2. Eyes   ☐   ☐

   ☐ fixates binocularly

   fixates with only one eye

   ☐ right   ☐ left

   ☐ looks at but cannot maintain fixation

3. Describe any other method of pointing used ____

_____

_____

_____

_____

_____

F. Uses facial expressions to communicate   ☐   ☐

Describe the expressions and what they indicate ____

_____

_____

_____

_____

_____

II. What kinds of things are communicated?

A. Present concerns   ☐   ☐

   ☐ desire for food   ☐ need for toileting

   ☐ desire for drink   ☐ discomfort or pain

   ☐ wants attention

Other _____

_____

_____

	YES	NO
B. Feelings	☐	☐

☐ happiness   ☐ humor
☐ sadness   ☐ love
☐ anger   ☐ frustration

Other _____

_____

| C. Offers or requests information | ☐ | ☐ |

☐ expresses ideas (give examples) _____

_____

_____

☐ offers suggestions (give examples) _____

_____

_____

☐ asks questions (give examples) _____

_____

_____

| D. Refers to other than present-time events | ☐ | ☐ |

☐ refers to events which occurred in the *past* (examples) _____

_____

_____

☐ comments on or asks questions about future events (examples) _____

_____

_____

III. Cognitive-perceptual functioning

    A. Visual modality

| | 1. Attends to visual stimuli | ☐ | ☐ |

        What kind? _____

        How long? _____

| | 2. Recognizes some people | ☐ | ☐ |

        Who? _____

How indicated? _____

_____

_____

	YES	NO
3. Recognizes common objects	☐	☐

Examples _____

How indicated? _____

_____

4. Recognizes small replicas of common objects ☐ ☐

Examples _____

How indicated? _____

_____

5. Recognizes pictures ☐ ☐

☐ family   ☐ animals
☐ self   ☐ objects

6. Can match

☐ object to object (give examples) _____

_____

_____

☐ object to picture (give examples) _____

_____

_____

☐ picture to picture (give examples) _____

_____

_____

☐ abstract forms

☐ circle to circle   ☐ triangle to triangle
☐ square to square   ☐ diamond to diamond

Other _____

B. Auditory modality

1. Attends to auditory stimuli ☐ ☐

What kind? _____

How long? _____

	YES	NO

2. Responds to speech ☐ ☐

    ☐ smiles when talked to
    ☐ recognizes mother's voice
    ☐ responds differently to pleasant and angry talking (give examples) _____

_____

_____

3. Responds to simple requests or instructions, e.g.,
"Look at (or point to)" or "where is?" ☐ ☐

people
    ☐ Daddy   ☐ Mommy
Other (list) _____

_____

Real objects (list) _____

_____

_____

Pictures (list) _____

_____

_____

4. Shows recognition of the following when the words are spoken
    ☐ own name
    ☐ names of family members (list) _____

_____

_____

    ☐ body parts (list) _____

_____

_____

concepts
    ☐ more   ☐ in   ☐ up   ☐ little
    ☐ big   ☐ out   ☐ down   ☐ one
    Action words (list) _____

_____

_____

C. Intellectual development

    1. Estimated   At Chronological   Test Used
        Mental Age   Age

_____

_____

_____

    2. Best areas of functioning _____

_____

_____

_____

IV. Physical Capabilities

  A. Mobility

    ☐ ambulatory (describe any aids needed) _____

_____

_____

_____

    ☐ uses wheelchair

    Other (describe) _____

_____

_____

  B. Head Control

    ☐ holds head erect
    ☐ can hold head erect but with difficulty
    ☐ head usually hangs down or to side
    ☐ can control head well enough to use a head stick for pointing

  C. Sitting

    Describe how child sits and any special seating equipment used

_____

_____

_____

_____

D. Speech mechanism

　1. Respiratory control

　　☐ has developed ability to control exhalation for speech production

　　☐ has inadequate speech breathing pattern

　2. Laryngeal control

　　☐ has difficulty coordinating exhalation and production of laryngeal tone

　　☐ has marked tension associated with phonation

　3. Control of oral structures

Note any persistent infantile oral reflexes (suckle, mouth opening, biting) _____

_____

_____

Check appropriate evaluation

	adequate	poor	very poor
lips	☐	☐	☐
mandible	☐	☐	☐
tongue	☐	☐	☐
palate	☐	☐	☐

Describe

　sucking _____

_____

　chewing _____

_____

　swallowing _____

_____

　drooling _____

_____

　4. What is the prognosis for development of intelligible speech?

_____

_____

E.   Arm – hand – finger control

　1. On a flat surface placed in front of child (as for a communica-

tion board) child can point with accuracy to a picture or a symbol in a

☐ 3 x 3 inch square

☐ 2 x 2 inch square

☐ 1 x 1 inch square

2. Consider the diagram below to be a tray of suitable width-length dimensions for the child.

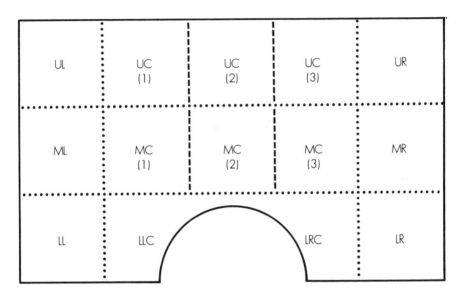

Observe the child point to pictures or objects placed in the various sections of the board and indicate the quality of the pointing by writing the appropriate letter in the space preceding the area listed below:

a. points accurately and quickly

b. points accurately but with effort

c. points in general area but could not specify more than 2 symbols in this area

d. points to general area but could not specify more than 1 symbol in this area

e. pointing is so inaccurate or is accompanied by so much involuntary movement or undesirable heightening of muscle tone that symbols should not be displayed in this area

LEFT	UPPER CENTER	MIDDLE CENTER	LOWER CENTER	RIGHT
☐ Upper (UL)	☐ (1)	☐ (1)	☐ Left (LLC)	☐ Upper (UR)
☐ Middle (ML)	☐ (2)	☐ (2)	☐ Right (LRC)	☐ Middle (MR)
☐ Lower (LL)	☐ (3)	☐ (3)		☐ Lower (LR)

V.   Social-emotional Development

   A. Interactions

      1. Seems to be content in the role of passive   YES NO
recipient of attention   ☐   ☐

      2. Initiates social interactions with others   ☐   ☐
         ☐ mother   ☐ father
         ☐ siblings (list) _____
         Others (list) _____

         _____

         Describe how social interactions are initiated _____

         _____

         _____

         _____

         _____

      3. Responds to efforts of others to initiate social
interactions   ☐   ☐
         ☐ mother   ☐ father
         ☐ siblings (list) _____
         Other (list) _____

         _____

         Describe how child responds _____

         _____

         _____

         _____

   B. What are the child's favorite activities? _____

         _____

_____

_____

_____

C. What are the child's particular dislikes? _____

_____

_____

_____

D. How does the child respond when others don't understand his efforts to communicate?

☐ persists but in a stereotyped way
☐ persists and tries different approaches
☐ gives up passively
☐ gives up but shows frustration

Analysis of inventory information

The information recorded on the preceding form might be summarized in many ways. Following are two methods of analyzing the information which offer guidelines for developing a symbol instruction program.

1. Processing of language-related stimuli

When organized to analyze how the child processes a language-related stimulus into a meaning, and how a response is formulated and executed, the summary provides important clues about communication problems and capabilities. A greatly simplified version of the steps between stimulus detection, message interpretation, response formulation and response production is diagrammed in Figure 2. Following is a brief description of the events taking place in each part of the internal aspect of the communication process.

Attending process (A in Figure 2). Sensory end organs are constantly bombarded by stimuli generated in the environment. From the end organ, the stimuli are transmitted to a buffer area in the central nervous system where they quickly decay. Only those stimuli on which attention is selectively focused are held and directed to appropriate areas for further processing. The child who cannot attend selectively to language-related visual stimuli such as Blissymbols must learn to do so before symbol learning can progress.

Visual processing 1 (B in Figure 2). Visual sensations are first analyzed for color and form. In this processing a visual stimulus is perceived as a line, a square, a circle or a star, for example. Processing at this level would enable the viewer to match pictures, words or other symbols but not to interpret their meaning.

Visual processing 2 (C in Figure 2). Following identification of color and form, the deeper meaning of visual stimuli is interpreted. Objects are identified and interrelationships among various aspects of the observed objects are interpreted. If the stimulus consists of written language, letters are discerned, combinations of letters forming a sentence are recognized. Other graphic, language-related stimuli such as Blissymbols are probably processed in a similar manner.

Auditory processing 1 (D in Figure 2). The sound wave is first processed as patterns of frequency, intensity and duration. Because of the transient nature of acoustic signals, a learner cannot study language-related sounds in the same manner as graphic (words or other symbols) visual stimuli because the latter may be kept in view for any desired length of time.

Auditory processing 2 (E in Figure 2). Sounds are recognized as noises, music or speech. If speech, the phonemes are detected and combined into syllables, words, phrases and sentences. Language rules may be applied to assist in interpreting the sound, since the acoustic form of the signal does not carry all the information needed to arrive at meaningful lexical, syntactic and semantic patterns.

Integration process (F in Figure 2). Information from the visual and/or auditory channels is brought together with incoming data from other senses and with stored information derived from previous experience. Meaning, based on the characteristics of the input and prior experience with similar input, is given to the stimulus. The words heard or the symbols seen are interpreted; thus, the language is comprehended and the message understood.

Ideo-motor process (G in Figure 2). Not all processed stimuli require an overt response. In fact, for most auditory and visual stimulation, processing ends with determination of meaning. When a response is to be made, the response must be formulated before a motor command is issued and executed. Perhaps the response will be "yes" or "no". It might be a comment or a question. The content and structure of responses varies with the responder's level of cognitive development and language learning.

Processing motor commands (H in Figure 2). Overt responses require appropriate neuro-muscular activity, which is initiated in the motor area of the cortex. For a spoken response, neural impulses are transmitted to the muscles that execute the movements of respiration, phonation and articulation. Manual responses — pointing, gesturing, writing — result from appropriate neural signals to muscles of the upper extremity. Eye movement and eye fixation responses are effected by neural signals to the extrinsic ocular muscles. One can see from this analysis how it might be possible for a child to have difficulty processing symbols (written or spoken words) that are referenced to speech sounds and yet be able to learn meaning-referenced visual symbols.

2. Characteristics of communication problem

Another useful analysis leads to a gross classification on the basis of three factors: understanding of spoken language, intelligibility of speech and ability to interpret visual stimuli. Summarized below in Figure 1 are the characteristics of four frequently encountered childhood communication problems.

Figure 1. Classification of some common communication problems

	Understanding of speech		Intelligibility of speech		Ability to interpret visual stimuli			
	Understands spoken language	Does not understand spoken language	Produces intelligible speech	Does not produce intelligible speech	Understands meaning of pictures	Does not understand meaning of pictures	Recognizes words	Does not recognize words
Type I	X		X		X			X
Type II	X			X	X			X
Type III		X		X	X			X
Type IV		X		X		X		X

Figure 2. Processing steps from detection of a language-related stimulus to an overt response

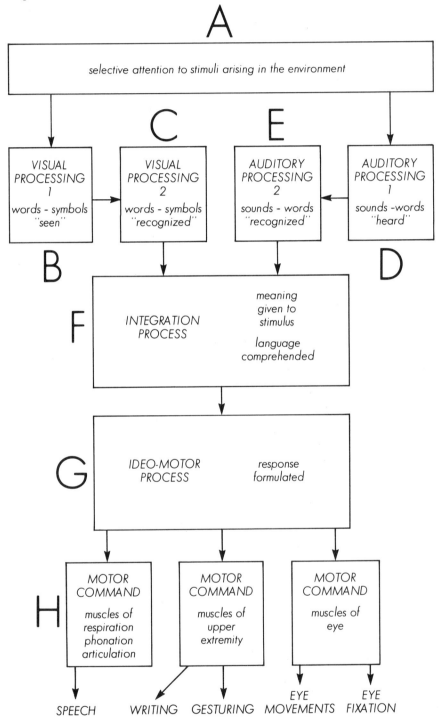

The Type I problem would probably be regarded as a reading disorder in a school-age child. Even though the child has intelligible speech, if difficulty in learning to read persists, an experimental period of Blissymbol training might be considered, especially in view of the child's ability to understand pictures.

The Type II problem is often classified as a language disorder but the ability to understand language suggests that the child needs to develop an expressive modality rather than improve receptive abilities. Since word recognition skills are absent, training the child to point to words displayed on a communication board is inappropriate. The child's ability to understand the meaning of pictures might be extended to interpreting pictographic Blissymbols. Symbol learning could be facilitated by the instructor's use of spoken language to explain symbol meanings.

The Type III problem differs from the Type II problem in that the child does not understand spoken language. However, the ability to understand pictures suggests that initiation of Blissymbol training would be appropriate. Although oral descriptions of symbol meaning should not be neglected, training should focus on developing symbol interpretation skills through the visual channel.

The Type IV problem is characterized by stimulus processing difficulties in both the auditory and visual modalities. It is extremely difficult to determine the intellectual potential of a child with a Type IV problem. Only through carefully designed and expertly conducted diagnostic teaching can the child's potential for learning be assessed. Such teaching would stress development of communication skills as well as stimulation of cognitive development. A child with this combination of problems would not be ready for Blissymbol training.

VIII. Teaching Blissymbolics to Children

Who will teach Blissymbolics to children who are unable to develop intelligible speech? Judging from the backgrounds of persons who have enrolled in Blissymbolics Training programs, a great variety of persons — teachers, speech/language pathologists, occupational therapists, aides, parents — many of whom have had little training in educational procedures. The purpose of this chapter is to provide guidelines for beginning symbol instruction and to offer illustrative teaching procedures.

Types of symbol instruction

Since the initial application of Blissymbolics at the Ontario Crippled Children's Centre in 1971, instructors have taught Blissymbolics in several ways. These are described in the *Handbook of Blissymbolics* (pp.89–92) as models for the application of Blissymbolics as an augmentative means of communication.

In *Model One* Blissymbolics is taught as an expressive modality to persons who have "fairly well established native language competence" in the receptive mode. When employing this model the symbol instructor can call attention to the composition of each symbol and explain the rationale on which the symbol is based. The symbol user can learn to employ Blissymbolics to its full potential, acquiring an extensive symbol vocabulary, and becoming skilled in the use of indicators and techniques for changing symbol meaning. After learning the system of Blissymbolics the child's expressive language level might become comparable to the receptive level.

In *Model Two,* Blissymbolics is taught to facilitate the expressive use of language and thus make possible more social interactions during the early stages of language development. This model might be used with young children whose cognitive development is progressing at a normal rate but who are at risk for development of oral expression. It might also be appropriate for some mentally retarded children. Symbol instruction would follow, though for some children at a slower pace, the sequences of normal language development. The normally developing child might reach the same level of symbol use as the Model One symbol learner. Retarded children should reach levels commensurate with their cognitive abilities. When teaching sentence construction to young or mentally retarded children, the symbol instructor will probably find that the word order of English will be easier for the children to learn and to use than the word order of Bliss syntax. In planning the teaching program the symbol instructor should bear in mind that Bliss syntax was designed for use by persons with a well-developed language system and, hence, might not be appropriate for the young or the mentally retarded learner.

In *Model Three,* Blissymbolics is taught to provide communication using surface-level language structures. Candidates for a Model Three approach are children functioning at low cognitive levels or those who have severely-impaired language processing capabilities. A symbol vocabulary representing words of high utility in everyday activities is taught. Some low functioning children can learn to produce simple sentences following stereotyped patterns.

The Blissymbolics Communication Institute emphasizes that these models have not been completely developed; however, they provide ''a provisional framework to facilitate assessment and programming of symbol communication for different populations.'' Study of the models also indicates that Blissymbolics may be appropriately taught to persons who present a variety of problems in developing communication skills. In other words, instruction in Blissymbolics should not be restricted to one type of communication problem such as cerebral palsy or mental retardation. Rather, it should be considered for any person who is unable to speak intelligibly regardless of the cause of the expressive disability.

Another way of interpreting these models is to think about whether the potential symbol user will employ symbols as a surface-level communication system only or be able to use deep-level structures also.

1. Blissymbolics as a surface-level communication system (corresponds to Model Three)

This is the way children with limited cognitive development or severe language learning problems learn to use symbols. Some acquire only a small symbol vocabulary of meanings that are highly functional in their real-life activities. Symbols are chosen and taught that enable the child to communicate about basic needs such as for food, drink, toileting, rest, nursing care, attention, and to express feelings such as happiness, sadness, love and anger. Children with a little higher level of cognitive development may also learn a few sentences that they will use repeatedly.

2. Blissymbolics as a deep-level expressive language system (corresponds to Models One and Two)

a. *Symbols may be used to express a developed or a normally developing receptive language* by children whose motor dysfunction precludes production of intelligible speech. Many cerebral palsied children, for example, have intact auditory functions (see A, D, E, F in Figure 2) that permit acquisition of the phonologic, morphologic, syntactic and semantic structures of language; yet they are unable to use speech for communication because of inadequate control of the speech-producing structures (see H in Figure 1). Depending on their intellectual development, these children may be expected to develop large symbol vocabularies, use techniques for generating new meanings, and construct different types of sentences as they communicate spontaneously in real-life situations.

b. *Symbol learning may parallel and contribute to development of language.* There are children who appear to have difficulty in processing the auditory signals of spoken language (See A, D, E, F, in Figure 2) and, as a result, have problems in learning to comprehend spoken language. Such children are often described as having delayed receptive language development. Because traditional orthography — the symbols used in printed words — is sound referenced, children who have difficulty processing auditory signals may also have problems in learning to read. At the time of this writing no studies of the effectiveness of Blissymbol training with children who have receptive language learning problems have been reported. It seems reasonable, however, to speculate that if receptively impaired children can grasp the meaning of pictographic and ideographic symbols they might be better able to interpret the auditory signals associated with the symbols, even though their perception of the auditory stimuli is distorted.

Teaching methods and teaching materials

Two factors must be considered when deciding *what* symbols and *what* syntax are to be taught and *how* the symbols and syntax are to be taught:

1. The language-processing capabilities of the potential symbol user.
2. How Blissymbolics will be used: whether as the expressive mode of a surface-level language system or to express deep-level language structures.

It is true that learning Blissymbolics has enabled some communicatively handicapped persons to express themselves and to function more effectively in interpersonal relations when they had been unable to develop intelligible speech or to learn to use conventional graphic symbols. It must be kept in mind, however, that Blissymbolics cannot be learned equally well by everyone, and that some persons may be unable to learn Blissymbolics because of such problems as severe intellectual impairment, poor vision, or severe central language processing deficiencies. The decision to exclude a child from symbol instruction should be weighed carefully. In view of the unique meaning-based characteristics of Blissymbols, it is recommended that decisions about a child's aptitude for learning to communicate with Blissymbols not be based on performance with conventional test materials. Not enough studies have been conducted to determine the relationship between levels of accomplishment on various psycho-educational tests and the learning of Blissymbols; therefore, it appears appropriate to propose that direct observation of how a child responds to Blissymbol instruction might be the best indicator of whether or not a child can learn Blissymbolics.

Blissymbols and stages of language development

In the absence of empirical data on which to base the sequences of Blissymbol training, logic would suggest following the major stages in the normal child's development of the expressive use of language.

1. One-word stage

The age at which normally developing children produce their first word varies from child to child but all children go through a period of expressing themselves in one-word utterances before moving to the two-word stage. The lexicon of a normal child in a normally stimulating environment expands rapidly and at two years of age the child might use 200 or more words. For the non-speaking child who uses language receptively it would not be appropriate to select for the initial teaching those symbols which represent the first words children speak. However, the fact that the first spoken words were used in relation to objects with which the child was familiar or events that were of personal significance does offer guidance for symbol selection.

The early symbol vocabulary should represent people with whom the child interacts, objects of special interest, actions that are part of the child's life and basic feelings that the child wants to express. Vocabularies selected in this manner for non-speaking children will have some common symbols but other items will be taught in response to the child's unique interests or needs. To encourage the child's expressive efforts, the first symbols taught should be for words the child is likely to use frequently. Following is a brief list of words that early school-age, non-speaking children find useful:

People
> *Common:* I, you, me, father, mother, brother, sister, grandpa, grand-
> ma, uncle, aunt, teacher
> *Special:* doctor, nurse, therapist

Objects
> *Common:* toilet, food, home, bed, drink
> *Special:* wheelchair, a pet, a toy

Actions
> *Common:* want, like, love, give, have
> *Special:* hurt

Feelings
> *Common:* happy, sad, angry
> *Special:* tired

Other
> *Common:* yes, no, hello, goodbye, thank you, you're welcome

The symbol learner should be encouraged to indicate objects, people, actions and feelings for which symbols are wanted. Suggestions for symbols to be taught should be solicited from parents, teachers and others with whom the child attempts to interact.

In the past it was believed that during the one-word stage children are developing only a ''naming'' skill, that is, that they are learning words that represent people, objects or actions, but not syntax. In view of the child's comprehension of sentences spoken by others it is now recognized that during this stage the child is also learning to analyze syntactic structure. When strings of one-word utterances produced during the latter part of the one-word stage are analyzed, it appears that in some strings the words are related to each other. This suggests that the child begins to use words in a way more complex than mere "naming" before achieving the ability to combine words into a two-word sentence. Such one-word sequences have been referred to as "vertical" constructions. There is an important implication in this observation for persons communicating with a symbol user — even though the child can indicate only one symbol at a time, don't assume that the child intends to use only one word to express the intended message. Wait *patiently* and with demonstrated *interest* to see if the child plans to produce a sequence of symbols. Even if a sequence of symbols does not result in a conventional sentence form, think about the possible relationships between the symbols used.

Another feature of some one-word utterances, having possible implication for teaching symbols to a handicapped child and for communicating with a symbol user, is their holophrastic nature. It has been reported frequently that children may use the same word to mean different things and even to represent complex ideas. For example, by pointing to a symbol for television the child might be indicating a desire to go to the room in which the television set is located. Only by questioning the child can the intent be determined. In other words the symbol represents something about the message but by itself is not the message.

2. Two-word stage

The first two-word utterances, such as "bye-bye," "all gone" actually function as one word. True semantic-syntactic relations appear when the child orders words to show relationships such as

agent – action:	"Nana go"
action – object	"Drink milk"
location – object:	"Here ball"
object – location:	"Doggie out"
possessor – possessed:	"Daddy hat"

Even though the syntax of these expressions is simple, the speaker's intended meaning is clear. It is important to remember that expanded sentences with correct grammar and mature syntax are not always essential for basic communication. Especially with non-speaking children of school age, the instructor may feel that correct grammar should be stressed. If the child's receptive language does not contain the syntax rules, it is advisable to focus on development of the lexicon and practice with two-word expressions before introducing grammar.

3. Telegraphic speech stage

Children do not progress directly from the two-word stage to a three-word stage nor to a multi-word stage in which all the parts of speech are used. Rather, for some time children produce short sentences of varying length which consist mainly of *content* words. Content words such as nouns and verbs carry meaning in themselves. At the beginning of this stage children do not use prepositions, conjunctions, articles, adverbs and adjectives. Auxiliary verbs are not used. Tense is indicated by a verb ending as in "I goed" instead of "I went." Similarly plurals are formed with an ending as in "mans" for "men."

Some low-functioning children are unable to progress beyond this level. Even though they have learned more advanced linguistic constructions, children with poor pointing ability may continue to use telegraphic expressions. If they are required to point to articles, prepositions, and other *function* words in addition to the *content* words, their communication will be slowed. Many people will not have the time nor patience to carry on the interaction. It would be unwise for the symbol instructor to insist on the use of sophisticated grammar at the expense of opportunities to interact with other people.

4. Function-word stage

In both spoken and written language many words are used which by themselves carry little meaning. Their function is to indicate the relationships among other words in the sentence. Included in the so-called "function" words are auxiliary verbs, prepositions, conjunctions, articles, and some adverbs and adjectives.

Blissymbolics includes symbols for many prepositions, articles, and conjuctions (see section on particles, page 42). The system does not symbolize auxiliary verbs. Through the use of the description (evaluation) indicator, adverbs and adjectives may be symbolized. In the system of Blissymbolics function words have only a minor role. Bliss argues that the meaning of some function words, specifically the particles, is ambiguous and often leads to misunderstanding.

The teaching of symbols for the function words should not be emphasized until the child has learned the symbols for many nouns and verbs, has used symbols in formulating telegraphic messages, and is communicating well using telegraphic constructions.

Acquisition of verb forms. The learning of verb forms follows a developmental sequence. Verbs undergo many inflections in response to the requirements of grammar. Familiarity with the order of acquisition will aid the symbol instructor in planning a teaching sequence.

Uninflected verbs, i.e., verbs with no modification in the base form are first used. These verbs refer to present time, as in "I play". Next the child adds the suffix "ing" to the base form, thus making a *present progressive* verb, as in "I playing". The addition of "s" to produce the proper present tense form when the subject of the verb is a singular noun or a third person pronoun is learned later. When representing present tense in Blissymbolics the same indicator is used to indicate the uninflected verb, present progressive and base form with the suffix "s":

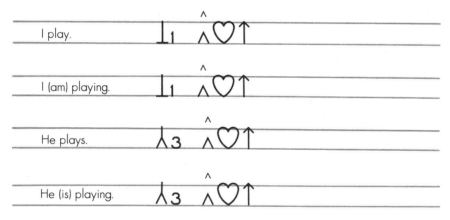

The verb forms "play," "playing," and "plays" are represented by the same symbol with the present tense shown by the action indicator.

Forms of the verb "to be" are among the last of the function words to be learned; hence it is likely that the child will think "I playing" before "I am playing" and "He playing" before "He is playing." Actually there is little difference in meaning among these present tense forms. At the time of this writing, Blissymbolics does not symbolize the various verb forms that appear in the normal sequences of language development. The teacher, therefore, must translate symbols for verbs in forms appropriate for the child's level of language development.

Past tense forms are learned after the present tense. It is more difficult for a child to understand that an action *has taken place* than to observe that an action *is taking place*. In written and spoken language the past tense of most verbs is indicated by adding the suffix "ed" to the base. These are referred to as *regular verbs*. To indicate past tense of other verbs the base form is changed, e.g., "eat–ate", "go–went" and "see–saw." These irregular forms are learned later than regular forms. When representing past tense in Blissymbols no distinction is made between regular and irregular forms. Both are symbolized by the past action indicator ⌐‾.

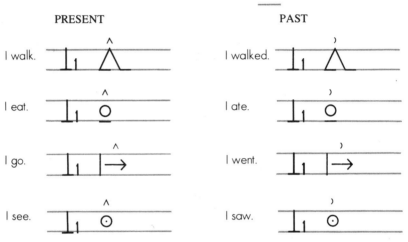

Future tense forms are even more abstract than past tense. It is easier for the child to understand that an action *has taken place* than to understand that an action *will take place*. In English we have many ways of indicating future time, e.g., "I am going to request permission," "I am requesting permission tomorrow," "Next week I request permission," "I shall request permission," "I'll ask for permission." While young children generally use the auxilliary verb "will" or its contraction as in "I'll" to express simple futurity, the instructor should keep in mind that the symbol user may also employ other locutions to indicate future time. Grammarians distinguish between proper use of "shall" and "will," however, in general usage, these distinctions are not made and "will" is used with all persons. The same contraction, "ll," is used for both *shall* and *will*. In Blissymbolics, futurity is expressed by the future action indicator, which does not distinguish between *shall* and *will:*

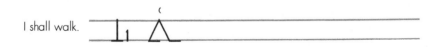

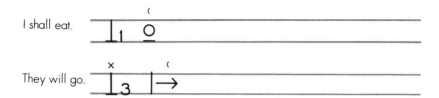

I shall eat.

They will go.

Forms of the verb "to be" as used in English grammar are difficult for some children to master and they are among the last of the function words to be acquired. The verb "to be" has been called a "defective" verb because its conjugational forms come from three unrelated stems. Correct use of the various forms of "to be" is confusing to the language learner. Further, while time is indicated by past tense forms (was and were), present tense forms carry little meaning, for example "I go" or "I going" convey the same meaning as "I am going" whereas "I was going" has a different meaning from "I going." Understanding of the verb "to be" is further complicated by its usage as a copula, or linking verb (I am hungry); as an auxiliary verb (I am eating an apple); or as a substantive verb (I am at home) in which "am" functions as a verb of complete predication to indicate "exist" or "live."

Bliss comments that the "verb 'to be' is one of the most important words in most languages. Indeed, without it we won't be able to form most sentences" *(The Book to the Film 'Mr. Symbol Man,'* p.83). He derives

ⓘ which means *being* from the larger symbol ⓘ which means *life*.

Tense is indicated by placing the appropriate indicator above the symbol:

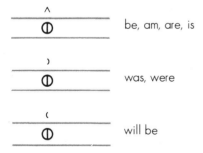

be, am, are, is

was, were

will be

Modal auxiliaries (can, could, may, might, should and would) are later-learned verb forms. These verbs are used in verb phrases and are not likely to be employed by the young symbol user or one whose limited cognitive functioning permits development of only a surface level communication system.

The Blissymbol for *can* is based on the assumption that the word "can" involves a human evaluation made before an action is attempted (see p.58):

I can push it.

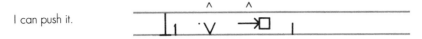

In general usage "can" and "could" are often used interchangeably although "could" carries an indication of time. In the sentence, "I showed I could do it" meaning "I showed I was able to do it" the verb "could" refers to past action. The verb "could" is also used to express conditionality as in "I could do it" which means "I should be able to do it".

The modal auxiliary "may" is represented by a small question mark placed above the verb to indicate its conditional status. This conditional indicator is translated as *may* or *might*.

He may/might walk.

Bliss uses the same conditional indicator to represent *would* as in

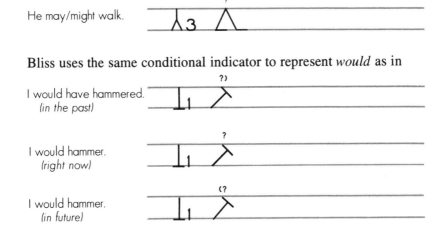

I would have hammered.
(in the past)

I would hammer.
(right now)

I would hammer.
(in future)

He notes that the verb in sentence number 1 could also be read I "may have hammered" and the verb in sentences 2 and 3 could be read I "may hammer" *(Semantography,* p.323). There is no symbol given in *Semantography* for the modal auxiliary "should."

For the instructor who wants to follow the developmental sequence of verb form acquisition, Blissymbolics will appear to be inadequate. The reader is reminded that Bliss strove to simplify grammar. He had no intention of paralleling English — or any other — grammar. While it would be difficult to teach all the verb forms using Blissymbols, it is easy to teach the concept of action, present, past and future, and the concept of conditionality:

Prepositions. Prepositions are words that indicate position, direction, time or an abstract relation. There is a large number of prepositions in

English but many of them are used only infrequently. The most commonly used are: in, on, at, by, to, for, from, with, of. Prepositions denoting location — "in" and "on" — are used first. The Blissymbols for these prepositions are easy for a child to understand.

the dot is *in* the box

the pointer is *on* the line

The symbols for *to* and *from* are also easy to explain:

the arrow is pointing *to* the line

the arrow is pointing away *from* the line

The rationale for the other commonly used prepositions is more difficult to explain to children (see pp.44-45):

>·   at   <   by, of   »   for

The preposition "with" creates many difficulties for the language learner. *Webster's New International Dictionary* lists twenty-two meanings or uses of "with." Bliss symbolizes two meanings of *with,* one in the sense of *and,* the other in the sense of *with the help of.* The sentence, "I work with father" might mean the same as "I and father work". *(Semantography,* p.439). This concept is represented by a half-size addition symbol drawn on the horizontal midline:

However, this symbol does not distinguish between the meanings "I work *with* father", i.e., I and father work *together* and "I and father work", i.e., each of us works but *not* together.

The sentence, "I work *with* a hammer" means, according to Bliss, "I work *with the help* of a hammer." This concept is represented by a half-sized addition symbol drawn on the skyline:

The symbol user may have difficulty representing such constructions as:

With all his toys he's still unhappy.

I'm *with* you on that!

The children were left *with* their uncle.

He played *with* skill

and the symbol instructor may need to help the child find other locutions to express these thoughts. For example, "With all his toys he's still unhappy" might be expressed as "He has a lot of toys but he is still unhappy." The sentence, "I'm with you on that!" might be expressed as "I agree with you." Some children simply use the Blissymbol for *with the help of* to represent those meanings of "with" other than in the sense of "and." They rely on the context to suggest the sense in which "with" is used.

5. Plurals

In English, nouns are inflected in several ways to indicate that the speaker means more than one (see p.35). Children begin to use noun inflections and verb inflections at about the same time — usually between two-and-a-half and three years of age. Some plural forms are not learned until children are of elementary school age. A child with a language learning problem is often confused by the many rules for forming English plurals. In Blissymbolics the rule is simplified — to indicate "more than one" place the plural indicator (a quarter-size $\overset{\times}{\rule{1cm}{0.4pt}}$) above the noun.

The same procedure is followed to indicate the plural of pronouns:

she or
her

they or
them

6. Questions

In English there are two common methods of asking a question.

a. Through the use of interrogative words:

Who ate the apple?
What should I do?
Where shall we go?
Which way did he go?
How are you?

b. By changing the order of subject and verb, so that the verb precedes the subject:

Was he there?
Are you in your place?

or so that the subject is between the auxiliary verb and the main verb:

Are you going?
Will you go?

At about two-and-a-half years children begin using interrogative words, as in "Where Daddy?" and between three and four years normally developing children ask questions beginning with "why," "what" and "how." Before learning to use interrogative words, the child might ask for an object or person by changing the intonation while speaking the word. Symbol instructors might teach children with retarded language development to

express a query by pointing to the symbol for question ⟨?⟩ and then

to the lexical item before teaching the other question forms.

When constructing questions in English, a question mark is placed at the end of the sentence. In Bliss syntax the symbol for question is placed at the beginning of the sentence:

Question   you   need   flag

When a question opens with an interrogative word, the symbol

| ? | is not used, since a question mark is the first element in the symbols for the interrogatives (see p.65).

Why   you   need   flag

$$\underline{?\triangleright \quad \underset{2}{\perp} \quad \overset{\wedge}{/} \quad \sqcap}$$

The symbols following the interrogative symbol are ordered as for a declarative sentence.

The expressions, "Question you need flag," and "Why you need flag," while clear in intent to the mature language user, might confuse the young or retarded language learner who is accustomed to hearing mature English spoken. The symbol instructor might need to clarify these questions by translating them into the English question form, which involves adding the auxilary verb "do" to the first sentence, thus making it "Do you need a flag?" and inserting "do" between the interrogative "why" and the pronoun "you" in the second sentence, making it "Why do you need a flag?" Such translation or interpretation might be indicated also when helping a symbol user learn English syntax.

7. Negative forms

Before they are a year old, normally developing children seem to understand and respond to "no" and at about the same time begin expressing negative reactions through gestures such as pushing things away and head shaking. To participate effectively in making decisions about matters which affect his life the child must be able to express refusal, denial and prohibition. There is an old saying to the effect that "Silence gives consent." Agreement, acceptance, affirmation are assumed unless a negative response is expressed. The symbol instructor should teach the symbol for *no* early in the symbol program. Semantically the words "no" and "not" are closely related. A dictionary definition of "not" is "a word expressing the idea of "no" and a dictionary definition of "no" is "not in any degree; not at all." *Not* is symbolized as ―| (*minus* with *intensity*) and *no* as ―|| (*not* with *intensity*). This rationale may be too abstract for young or retarded learners to understand, but they can learn to use this symbol by associating it with gestures of negation such as head shaking and pushing away an unwanted object. Children's first negative statements consist of the word ''no'' used alone. The one word negative response ''no'' continues to occur frequently in everyday oral communication. During the early stages of language development children also construct negative statements by placing ''no'' at the beginning of a sentence, for example:

No wash hands.
No touch.
No eat.

At a later stage the negative may be preceded by a subject, for example:

I no wash hands.
Baby no touch.
Doggie no eat.

Use of auxiliary plus the negative ''not'' and the contracted forms appear later:

I will not (won't) wash my hands.
Baby do not (don't) touch.
Doggie is not (isn't) eating.

In written negative statements using Bliss syntax, the negative is placed before the verb:

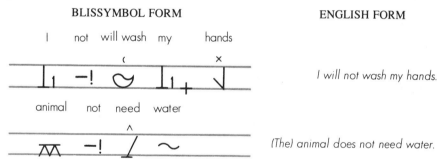

BLISSYMBOL FORM

I   not will wash my   hands

I will not wash my hands.

ENGLISH FORM

animal   not need water

(The) animal does not need water.

This word order is not the same as that of mature English but is similar to that used in an early stage of language learning. It is essential for the symbol instructor to realize that children progress through several stages in learning the correct English syntax for negative statements and negative questions. Before introducing the mature syntactic forms to young or retarded children the symbol instructor should provide opportunities for them to express negation using symbol order appropriate for their level of language development.

8. Passive voice

The inflection of verbs which identifies the subject as the *doer* or the *receiver* of the action is called "voice." When the subject is the *doer* the voice is *active*, when the subject *receives* the action the voice is *passive*. While children begin using this form between two-and-a-half and three years of age, in expressions such as:

Her gets spanked.

The dog got wet.

they apparently do not learn how to formulate passives until later. Bliss does not encourage use of the passive form but he has devised a simple procedure for symbolizing it (see p.66):

1. Write the symbol for the receiver of the action as the subject.
2. Place the passive indicator above the verb with the point toward the subject.
   a. Use no other action symbol for present tense.
   b. For other tenses use both the passive symbol and appropriate tense marker.

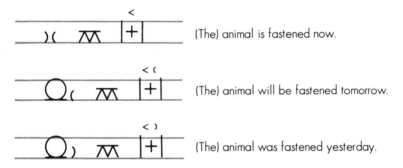

(The) animal is fastened now.

(The) animal will be fastened tomorrow.

(The) animal was fastened yesterday.

Since use of the passive is more important as a matter of style than of grammar this form should not be taught until the child has acquired most of the other grammatical forms.

Outline of developmental sequences of receptive and expressive language acquisition

It is not within the scope of this book to review in detail the sequences of language development, although a detailed knowledge of language acquisition would aid the symbol instructor in program development. It will be some time before well-trained language specialists are available to serve all persons who need assistance in developing communication skills. In the meantime, Blissymbolics will be taught by persons whose backgrounds do not include training in teaching language. It is not our intention to discuss how to help a child develop language. Rather, our objective is to consider how to teach a child to express, using Blissymbols, what language has been acquired. Not all of the forms that occur in the normal developmental sequence can be expressed in Blissymbols. This is not a criticism of Semantography. We reiterate our earlier comment that Bliss strove to create a symbol system to be used by persons with *mature* language development. He deliberately chose a simple grammar. The grammar of English is anything but simple, with its many verb forms, plural forms, etc. Blissymbolics is not — and was not intended to be — a system for teaching all the grammatical forms that children learn as they progress through the normal developmental sequences. It follows, then, that in using an outline of the developmental sequences of receptive and expressive language acquisition the symbol instructor should not look for Blissymbols to express every form the language learner acquires. Such an outline can, however, provide general guidelines by indicating the nature of receptive and expressive language characteristic of the various developmental stages.

OUTLINE OF DEVELOPMENTAL SEQUENCES OF RECEPTIVE AND EXPRESSIVE LANGUAGE ACQUISITION (AGES ARE ONLY APPROXIMATE)

At about 12 months
>Receptive:
>>Recognizes own name and names of familiar people and objects
>>Understands ''yes'' and ''no''
>>Responds to ''bye bye''
>Expressive:
>>Speaks first word and may have vocabulary of 6 words of noun type.

Between 12 and 18 months
>Receptive:
>>Follows simple commands (give, kiss)
>>Recognizes one body part (usually eyes or nose)
>Expressive:
>>Has a vocabulary of about 20 words, predominately nouns but some verbs (e.g., see, want, go), and some adjectives (e.g., big, more)

Between 18 and 24 months
>Receptive:
>>Identifies five body parts

Recognizes names of more objects and persons

Can identify some pictures and is beginning to match some objects with their pictures

Expressive:

Vocabulary now about 100 words, including nouns, verbs, adjectives, adverbs and a few personal pronouns (I, me, you)

Produces two word phrases in 'telegraphic' form such as:

Agent-action ....''mommy eat''
Action-object ....''wash dollie''
Location-object ....''here doggie''
Possessor-possessed ....''daddy shoe''
Attribute-object ....''big bed''

Between 24 and 30 months

Receptive:

Understands complex sentence forms

Understands some prepositions (in, on, under)

Distinguishes between action words (come-go, run-stop, give-take)

Identifies actions in pictures

Understands concept of ''one'' and ''many''

Expressive:

Many words — vocabulary increases to 200–300 words

Beginning to use question forms — ''Where Daddy?''

New word forms: articles (a, the) conjunctions (and)

Between 30 and 36 months

Receptive:

Acquiring lexical items at a rapid rate — the number of words understood reaches about 800 during this period

Understands ''big-little''

Identifies 7 body parts

Comprehends most sentence structures

Expressive:

Uses some pronouns (I, it, this, my, mine)

Use some verb inflections

copula ''is'' (or 's in such sentences as ''He's out.'')

is + verb + ing

regular past ''ed''

Beginning to use plural form of nouns, the possessive form, and prepositions beginning with indicators of position or location

Between 36 and 48 months

Receptive:

Understands about 1500 words

Comprehends compound and complex sentences

Understands sex difference pronounce (he, she, him, her)

Expressive:

Number of words used is from 900 to 1500

Constructs multi-word sentences including compound, complex, imperative

Sentences are less telegraphic, that is, they contain more function words

Asks questions using "why," "what," "where," "how"

Uses pronoun "we"

Between 48 and 60 months

Receptive:

Understands 1500 to 2000 words

Comprehends sentences containing dependent clauses beginning with "if," "because," "when"

Expressive:

Uses approximately 2000 words

Uses more verb forms

Between 60 and 72 months

Receptive:

Understands 2500 to 2800 words

Can comprehend all but the most complex syntactic structures, including passive voice

Expressive:

Uses approximately 2500 words

Uses a variety of syntactic structures with only occasional errors in grammar

Uses correct forms of the verb, "to be," and most irregular verbs

Uses prepositions "to" and "of"

In using this outline the reader is cautioned that the breakdown into periods of six or twelve months is arbitrary. There is no specific age at which children begin using a particular grammatic form or language structure and there is marked variability in the rate of language acquisition among children of normal intelligence. In general, regardless of their rate of language learning, most children seem to follow the same sequences. Mentally retarded children with no specific language learning problem acquire language at a slower rate. Children who can not learn to speak intelligibly may or may not be mentally retarded. Also they may or may not have difficulty developing receptive language. If a child's comprehension of language is appropriate for his level of intellectual functioning, the Blissymbol training program should focus on teaching the symbols needed for that developmental level. When development of receptive language is delayed or impaired, symbols might be helpful in the child's understanding of language.

Introducing symbols to the symbol learner

Selection of the teaching method to be used with a child should take into consideration the child's level of cognitive function, level of language development and characteristics of visual and auditory processing.

For the child whose cognitive development is normal for age, whose visual and auditory functions are intact but whose speech is unintelligible because of neuromuscular dysfunction, discussion of the symbols might facilitate their learning and use. The extent to which the symbol instructor explains the rationale of the symbols and the system would depend on the child's age. For children functioning at low cognitive levels and children who have impairment of auditory processing, such explorations would only be confusing. Following are some suggestions for introducing symbols to children with delayed language or cognitive development. Adaptations of these procedures may be useful with other children.

1. Introducing symbols for things and persons

a. Attach a symbol to the common object it represents. Use large drawings of the symbol (see *Appendix B* to learn how to enlarge symbols) or the flash cards available from BCI. Periodically call the children's attention to the symbol and the object it stands for. Speak the name of the object while pointing to the symbol. Gradually the children will make the desired association between the symbol and the object. Start with two pictographic symbols such as *chair* and *table*. Remove the labels and as you display them one at a time have the child point to the appropriate object. Then point to the object and have the child select by some method (for example, hand pointing or looking at) the appropriate symbol. When the child demonstrates that he or she has learned the two symbols, follow this procedure as you gradually add other pictographs appropriate for age such as *glass, clock window, pencil, book, bowl* (container).

b. On a large doll or picture of a person attach over the eye and over the nose the symbols for *eye* and *nose*. Remove the labels and as you show them to the child one at a time have the child point to eye or nose as appropriate. Then point to the eye or the nose and have the child indicate the appropriate symbol. When these symbols are consistently associated with the appropriate body part add, one at a time, the symbols for *ear, mouth, arm, legs and feet*.

c. On a large picture of a house attach the symbol for *house* and on a large picture of a tree attach the symbol for *tree*. Proceed as in a and b above. In this manner teach the symbols for woman, boy, girl, baby.

d. Where possible have the father wear the symbol for *father* and the mother wear the symbol for *mother*. Have father remove mother's symbol, show it to the child and request the child to point to or look at *mother*. Do this several times, then follow the same procedure with father. After the child learns to look appropriately when shown the symbol have both parents sit in front of child wearing their symbols. Remove the symbols and one at a time display them for the child and have the child point to the parent to whom the symbol refers.

Obtain photographs of father and mother and, if necessary, teach child to associate correct picture with each parent. This can be done with the procedure described for teaching the father and mother symbols. After the child consistently recognizes each picture fix them where the child can see them (perhaps on the wheelchair tray or on a desk top). Attach the father and mother symbols above their photographs. Hold a symbol for father before the child while asking the child to point to the picture of *father*. Do the same with *mother*.

2. Introducing symbols for action

a. To teach the action symbol *(to) walk* draw a large (12 inch high) symbol for *legs and feet* on stiff paper and a three-inch-high *action indicator* on a separate piece of stiff paper. Demonstrate to the child that the large symbol for *legs and feet* is the same as the symbol for *legs and feet* attached to the doll or picture in the labeling procedure used to teach the symbols for things. Attach the large legs and feet symbol to your skirt or slacks and while standing still before the child call attention to the symbol and to your motionless legs and feet. Then hold the action indicator above the legs and feet symbol and begin walking toward the child. Place two cards before the child, one with a large symbol for *legs and feet* only, the other with a large drawing of the *legs and feet* symbol and the appropriately positioned *action indicator*. Stand still before the child and point to your legs and feet. Ask the child to point to the correct symbol. Walk toward the child and ask the child to point to the correct symbol. When the child learns to point appropriately to the symbol for walking, associate the symbols with pictures of a person standing and walking.

b. To teach the action symbol *(to) bite,* first teach the pictographic symbol for *teeth* using a drawing or picture of a face with the teeth exposed. Hold the symbol for teeth beside your exposed teeth. Hold a card on which an appropriate size action indicator has been drawn so that the action indicator is positioned above the teeth symbol. Make a biting (not a chewing) action to bite off a piece of cookie or apple. After several demonstrations, place the symbols for *teeth* and for *(to) bite* in front of the child and have him point to the correct symbol as you expose your teeth or bite a cookie.

c. To teach the action symbol that means *(to) give,* review or teach the symbol for *bowl,* using a bowl that resembles the shape of the pictographic symbol for *container* (a half circle). On the palm of your right hand draw (with a lipstick or an eyebrow pencil) an arrow with the arrow head pointed toward the fingers and draw the action indicator above the arrow head on the middle finger as illustrated in Figure 3-A. Draw the container symbol on the bowl.

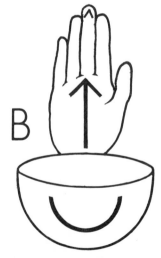

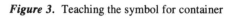

Figure 3. Teaching the symbol for container

Put some pieces of cookie or candy or some small toys in the bowl and place it on the tray or desk in front of the child. Hold your right hand with palm forward and fingers up behind the bowl as illustrated in Figure 3. Call the child's attention to the symbol elements by tracing them with a finger of your left hand. Reach into the container with your right hand and take an item between your thumb and first finger. Again hold your hand behind bowl so that the child can see the arrow and action indicator. As you say "give," give the item to the child by extending your hand so that the child can see the arrow moving toward him. Repeat many times. Then hold your right hand behind the bowl as shown. Take an item from the bowl with your left hand and slowly move it along the arrow while saying "give" and present it to the child with your left hand. After many presentations, place before the child a large symbol for *container* and a large symbol for *(to) give*. Provide the child with practice in pointing to the correct symbol to indicate that the child wants you to give him or her something.

d. To teach the action symbol that means *(to) love,* draw a 6 inch high heart symbol with the action indicator on stiff paper. Cut a 4-inch vertical slit in the heart as shown in Figure 4-A. On another piece of stiff paper (15 x 3 inches) draw an arrow with the straight line 12 inches long, as shown in Figure 4-B. From the back of the heart slip the arrow head through the slot, thus making the symbol for *(to) love* as shown in Figure 4-C.

Sit in front of the child and, while holding the symbol for *(to) love* over your heart, call the child's attention to the symbol as you smile and say

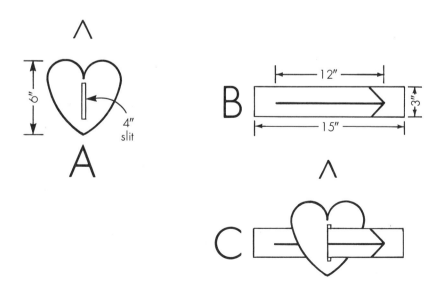

Figure 4. Teaching the symbol for to love

"love." Hold the symbol where the child can see it and act affectionately — hug, touch — point to the symbol and say "love." After several demonstrations, sit in front of the child and, while the child watches, push the arrow back and forth through the slot with the arrow head pointing toward the child. Accompany this action with repetitions of the word "love" and demonstrations of affection.

Display the symbols for *(to) give* and *(to) love*. Ask the child to point to a symbol. If he points to *give*, give a small toy. If he points to *love*, hug the child. You say one of the words. If the child points to the correct symbol, respond by giving a toy or by hugging.

Display the symbols for *(to) love* and *(to) bite* and proceed as above, giving a bite of cookie or a hug as appropriate.

Where possible, have the father and mother go through all these sequences for teaching the symbol *(to) love* to the child. If they are not available, arrange for some other person the child likes to use these procedures to help the child grasp the meaning of the symbol.

3. Introducing symbols for feelings

To teach the symbols for *happy* and *sad* use a 6 inch high heart drawn as for teaching *(to) love*, but with the *evaluation indicator* instead of the *action indicator*. On a 3 inch x 9 inch piece of stiff paper draw a 6 inch arrow. Pin the *heart* symbol over your heart. From a bag take a bright new toy. While holding the toy in one hand, laugh and say "happy" as you hold the arrow with point up beside the heart as in the symbol for *happy*. Put the toy in the bag and take the arrow away. From the bag take a broken toy. Look sad while you hold the broken toy. Pretend to cry and say "sad" as you hold the arrow, point down beside the heart as in the symbol for *sad*.

Place before the child the symbol for *happy* and the symbol *sad* and ask the child to point to the appropriate symbol when you laugh and look happy and when you pretend to cry and look sad. Say the word when the child points to the appropriate symbol. Use drawings or pictures of happy faces and sad faces and have the child point to the appropriate symbol as you display a picture. Say the word "happy" or "sad" when the child points to the correct symbol.

Ask the parents to describe some things that make the child happy and some that make him sad. Use these situations to develop ways of teaching the meaning of the *happy* and *sad* symbols. For example, if riding in the car makes the child happy and having to sit in a corner makes him sad these actual situations might be photographed and the pictures used to associate with the symbols.

Display on the child's communication board the symbols for *happy* and *sad* and ask the child each day to show you how he feels. Read a story and ask how he thinks someone in the story feels. Describe situations which would make the child feel happy and situations which make him feel sad and ask him how he would feel in that situation.

Practice in using symbols

Many procedures have been developed by symbol instructors to provide a variety of experiences with symbols (See *Handbook of Blissymbolics*, p.140–203). Following are a few illustrations of how Blissymbols might be used in games and various classroom activities. These illustrations will suggest adaptations and other activities to the symbol instructor.

1. Games

Bliss Bingo. Played by several persons using Bingo-like cards on which Blissymbols have been drawn instead of numbers. The teacher gives the meaning for a symbol. If a player's card has that symbol it is covered by a chip. As in Bingo, the first person to completely cover a row or column is the winner. From time to time new cards should be constructed in order to provide practice with new symbols. If a child can't place the chip on his card the teacher may help after the child indicates the location of the symbol. This might be done using a scanning technique or the child's card could be number and color coded for eye pointing (see p.148).

Bliss Concentration. This game may be used to teach children to match symbol to symbol or to match symbol and meaning. It may also be used to help other persons learn symbols. For symbol-to-symbol matching, draw two identical sets of symbols using a $2^5/8$ inch square as the scale on 3 inch x 3 inch square cards. The flash cards (see p.167) would provide a model, or you might use two sets of flash cards. Begin with eight pairs of pictographs such as *man, woman, table, chair, house, eye, ear, nose*. (The number of pairs used will depend on the cognitive level of the players). Punch a hole in each card so it can be hung on a display board. The display board might be an 18 inch x 18 inch piece of $1/4$ inch plywood with small nails or picture hangers spaced for hanging the cards. The board should be divided into rows which are colored and columns which are numbered (see Figure 5).

In playing the game the pairs of symbol cards are hung randomly on the

Figure 5. Layout for Bliss Concentration Game (Dots represent small nails or picture hangers for hanging Blissymbol cards)

	1	2	3	4	
RED	•	•	•	•	RED
YELLOW	•	•	•	•	YELLOW
BLUE	•	•	•	•	BLUE
GREEN	•	•	•	•	GREEN
	1	2	3	4	

display board with their backs toward the players. Player one indicates which card he wants turned over by giving a color–number code such as "red–three," then he selects one which he thinks will match, for example, blue–two. If they match, the pair is removed from the display board and placed in that player's pile and the player takes another turn. If they don't match, the two cards are turned with their backs to the players and player two takes a turn. The player with the greater number of cards in his pile at the end of the game is the winner.

To enable non-speaking children to indicate their selections, a display of the colors and numbers should be provided so they can point or signal with eyes and hands.

Variations of the procedures may be made after the children learn to play, using simple matching of symbols to achieve different teaching-learning objectives.

1. Using objects or pictures which represent the same meaning as the symbols, the child must identify the meaning of each symbol he pairs or the cards go into a neutral pile rather than into his pile, and don't count toward his score.

2. The teacher selects symbols that can be arranged to form sentences, for example, *I, you, see, have, eat, have, food, pencil*. The winner is the first child who can form a three-word sentence from the symbols he has matched, for example:

I see you.
I have pencil.
I eat food.

"Bliss Concentration" is a useful teaching-learning game because it

1. develops attending skills;
2. strengthens visual memory;
3. develops visual discrimination;
4. provides opportunities for social interaction;
5. helps the child learn to take turns and to follow rules;
6. can be modified for different levels of cognitive ability and language development.

2. Books

Personal symbol picture dictionary. Provide a three-ring binder and a supply of blank $8^{1}/_{2}$ inch x 11 inch three-hole paper for the child. As symbols are introduced, draw or cut pictures from magazines to illustrate the meanings represented by a symbol. Draw the symbol at the top of a page and paste the picture under the symbol. This is a good project for eliciting parental participation. Father and Mother should be asked to spend time at home with the child looking through magazines to find pictures to represent a symbol. After a child has learned the *house* symbol, for example, the teacher might draw the symbol for *house* at the top of a blank page and ask the parents to spend some time with the child at home looking through magazines. When the child sees a picture of a house the parent cuts it out and pastes it on the page. Pictures of different types of houses will broaden this concept and strengthen the child's understanding of the symbol. Provide opportunities for the child to show his dictionary to other people.

Stories. Children's stories can be modified by pasting an appropriate Blissymbol over words in the story. For example, in the sentence, "The gingerbread man ran down the hill" symbols might be used as follows:

The ginger ⬭ ∧ ran ↓ the hill.

Later symbols for *ran* and *hill* might be added and still later the symbol for *the*. It is easy to make these changes by drawing the symbols on self-adhesive correction tape which is available at office supply stores.

Encourage parents to purchase small, inexpensive children's books and read and reread the story to the child. After the child becomes familiar with the story select from the symbols the child has learned one that represents an important word in the story and draw it on a card or select it from a BCI flashcard. When reading the story show the card to the child whenever that word is said. Ask the child to look at or point to the symbol. When the child learns to do this, paste the symbol over the word in the book. Introduce other symbols in this way. Teacher and parents periodically read the story while the child looks at the book with them. The reader should ask the child to point to the symbol when that word is read. If the child can't point, the reader should point to the symbol as the word is said. As the child learns new symbols they should be added to the story and new story books should be obtained for the child — preferably by the parents. Ask the child to share his books with classmates but reinforce the idea that the book is the child's personal property. Encourage the child to "collect" books.

3. Bulletin Boards

Symbols for days of the week, months of the year, weather and special days may be taught and used through the real-life activity of putting the appropriate symbols on a bulletin board at the beginning of each day. Discuss the day and have the children select the appropriate symbols to be displayed. Encourage parents to do this on weekends and during school vacations.

4. Schedules

Symbols relating to on-going events in the child's life may be taught and reinforced by making individualized schedule cards. On each card should be a drawing of a clock showing a particular time and a sentence showing what the child does at that time, as illustrated in Figure 6.

Additional cards can be made to show the scheduled time for other activities in the child's life — therapy, listening to stories, going to bed, etc. Put the child's name on each card to help him become aware that this is a

Figure 6. Schedule Cards

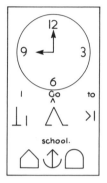
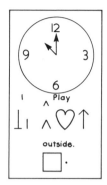
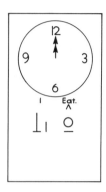
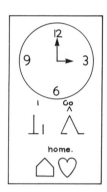

personal schedule. Suggest to the parents that schedule cards be developed for activities in the home. Not only does this activity help the child learn symbols but it contributes to development of self and time concepts.

Guidelines for teaching symbols

There is no one way to teach symbols. Imaginative symbol instructors will create many methods for helping children understand the meaning of symbols and will adjust their teaching procedures as the child responds. Such individualizing of instruction is encouraged and the following suggestions are offered as guidelines:

1. Symbol teaching should be related to meaningful everyday experiences of children.
2. Symbols should be made to serve a purpose for the child and not used merely in teaching-learning exercises.
3. A child needs varied experiences with a symbol in order to make it part of his language.
4. The instructor should be alert to the child's ideas, feelings and questions and provide symbols for expressing them.
5. Significant other persons in the child's community should be routinely involved in the child's learning and use of symbols.

Two sections of the *Handbook of Blissymbolics* offer additional information about teaching methods and materials: a program of symbol instruction is described on pages 140–218. Teaching aids and materials for the preschool and older symbol users, toys, games and aids to programming are discussed on pages 310–369. The *Newsletter* also publishes information about teaching methods and materials.

IX. Accessing Symbols

Methods of indicating symbol selection

Obviously symbols cannot help a child communicate unless they are easily accessible. To be of use in communication the individual symbols in a symbol display must be so located that the symbol user can indicate which symbol is to be noted by the observer. This is not difficult for symbol users whose control of arms and hands permits precise pointing to the symbol. These users can employ the direct selection technique. Many children who are unable to develop intelligible speech are also unable to develop adequately precise pointing. For them coding or scanning procedures make many symbols accessible by selection techniques requiring only minimal neuromuscular control.

1. Direct selection

The symbol user indicates a symbol in the display by touching it with a finger, a head pointer or by fixing his or her eyes on it. Direct selection is the shortest, most straightforward way of letting an observer know what symbol has been chosen in formulating the expression of the message. In mechanical or electro-mechanical devices there is a key or sensor for each of the symbols available to the user. Direct selection is used in producing a message on a typewriter. The typist operates an individual key for each letter in the message.

2. Coding

A code is a system in which meanings are assigned to letters, numbers, words or other symbols. For example, the Morse Code uses dots and dashes to represent the letters of the alphabet. In everyday use, codes are used to procure brevity or secrecy in a message. Coding permits transmission via various media and the holding of information in various types of memory or storage devices. Message transmission through a code requires encoding by the sender and decoding by the receiver; hence, both sender and receiver must know the code. Two simple codes can greatly increase the amount of information a severely handicapped person can express with a few gross movements.

Linear coding. Symbols in the display are numbered in sequence beginning with 1 (see Figure 7). The digits 0 through 9 are displayed where the child can touch each digit with a finger, headstick or in some other way indicate a number. For symbols numbered between 1 and 9 the child need point to only one digit. For symbols numbered between 10 and 99 the child would point to two digits, and to indicate a symbol numbered 100 or above the child would point to three digits. Suppose that in a child's display *I* is 1, *want* is 30 and *cookie* is 129. The child would point to 1 and move the hand to a specified area of the board to signify the end of that number. After the observer said "I", the child would point to 3 then 0 and signify the end of that number. After the observer said 'want' the child would point to 1, 2 and 9 and then signify the end of that number thus completing the message:

1 – 3, 0 – 1, 2, 9

I   want   cookie

Figure 7. Layout for linearly coded communication board (The child's symbols are drawn to the right of the numbers)

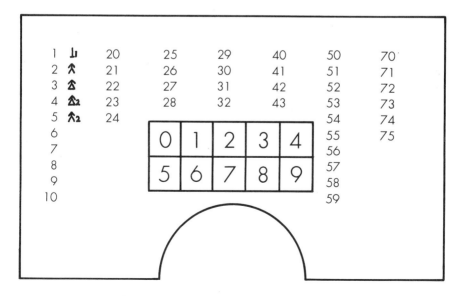

Figure 8. Layout for two-step coded communication board (The child's symbols would be drawn in the squares making up the matrix)

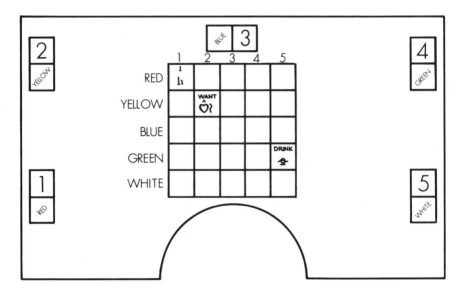

Two-step coding. Symbols in the display are arranged in rows and columns forming a matrix (see Figure 8). Usually the rows are colored and the columns are numbered. Pairs of numbers and colors are arranged around the periphery of the communication board in positions where the child can fix his gaze on them. The pairs must be far enough apart that the observer can detect at which one the child is looking. The child is taught to look first at a color. When the observer names the correct color the child then looks at a number. The observer says the number and then decodes the message. If a child using the display illustrated in Figure 8 first looked at red, then 1, the first symbol would be *I*. If the child next looked at yellow, then 2, the second symbol would be *want*. By looking at green, then 5, the child would complete the symbol message, *I want drink*.

3. Scanning

An indicator such as a finger, a light or a pointer traverses the display of symbols in sequence, pointing them out one by one. When the indicator is located at the selected symbol the child signals in some manner such as nodding his head or activating a switch. In the simplest form of scanning, the observer points to each symbol and the child indicates when the symbol wanted is touched. In electro-mechanical systems there is a small light bulb at each symbol location. The bulbs light in sequence. As a bulb comes on the preceding one goes off; thus, the child observes a light scanning the symbols. When the light appears at the desired symbol the child activates a switch to stop the scanning and hold the light at that point.

Formats for symbol displays

When arranging a symbol display for a child who will point with hand, headstick or eyes the child's control of movements must be carefully considered. In the chapter on assessment (pp.95-115) a procedure is described for observing and recording how well a child can point to various areas on a flat surface placed before him. Analysis of these observations will suggest how large the symbols should be and where they should be placed. Children who can point accurately may use small symbols arranged close together and may have many symbols in their display. Children who can point only with a fisted hand will need larger symbols and greater spacing between them.

The natural tendency is for a symbol instructor to arrange the symbols in neat rows on a rectangular tray. This arrangement works well for children with good pointing skills. Children with impaired upper extremity control or children who point with headsticks cannot reach all sections of a rectangular board; hence they would not have access to symbols placed out of their reach. Several individualized layouts are illustrated in Figures 9, 10 and 11.

Figure 9. Placement of symbols for a child who could not point to the left side of the tray

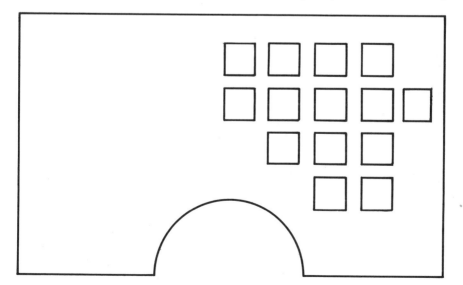

Figure 10. Placement of symbols for a child who could not point to the right side of the tray

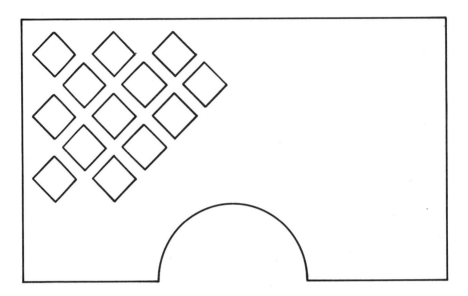

Figure 11. Placement of symbols for a child who used a headstick which he could move in an arc but could not extend into corners of tray

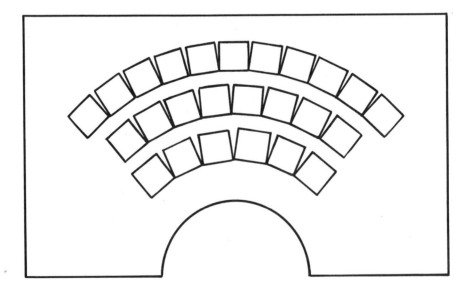

The Fitzgerald Key

The Fitzgerald Key was developed in 1926 for Edith Fitzgerald, a teacher in a school for the deaf, to teach language principles and sentence structure to deaf children. The system was designed to teach children to analyze the functional relationships among the parts of a sentence and understand how word order affects the meaning of a sentence. The use of visual cues which provide a visual pattern for correct word order is emphasized in this approach to language teaching. Words are placed in columns according to their grammatical form. The system as designed allows for analysis or construction of complex syntactic forms.

The Fitzgerald Key may be readily adapted to serve as a basis for arranging symbols in a symbol display. Initially symbols might be grouped into these categories:

who: *I, mother, father, teacher, brother, sister, you*
action: *want, have, go, love*
what: *food, drink, toy, letter, book, TV*
where: *home, toilet, school*
when: *how, today, tomorrow, weekend*

Later a column of "little words" might be added, which would include the symbols for articles *a, the;* the prepositions *to, for, at, in, on;* the

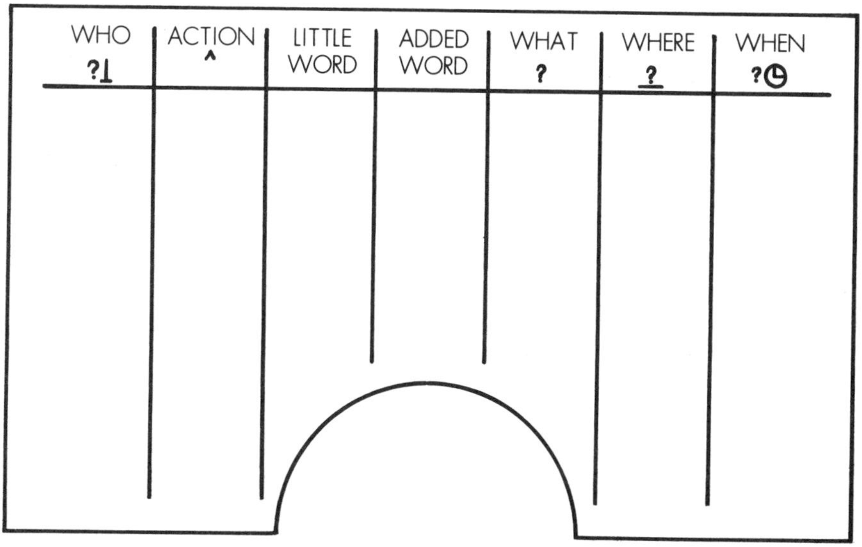

Figure 12. Layout for grouping symbols in format of an adaptation of the Fitzgerald Key

conjunction *on;* and the negative *not.* As a child's vocabulary increases and language development progresses a column "added words" (descriptions or evaluations) is added, for example, the symbols, *big, little, good, bad, happy, sad.* The layout of a display arranged in a manner of an adapted Fitzgerald Key is illustrated in Figure 12.

Constructing symbol displays

For non-ambulatory children symbol displays are constructed to fit on a wheel-chair tray, a desk top or lap tray. Construction should be kept as simple as possible to permit additions to the display as the child's symbol vocabulary grows and his knowledge of sentence structure advances. A stiff paper such as poster board cut to the size of the child's tray provides a good surface on which to affix the symbols. The display should be protected by a piece of plexiglass cut to the size of the tray and attached to permit easy removal for adding or rearranging symbols. The method (direct selection, coding, scanning) to be used by the child will determine the layout of the display.

1. Layout for direct selection

After studying the record of the child's pointing capabilities (see page 98) symbols should be place at those locations where the child can point most precisely. Before sticking the symbols to the poster board it is advisable to lay them on the poster board and cover them with a piece of plexiglass to allow experimenting with symbol positions and to keep the display clean and dry.

2. Layout for linear coding

When using the linear coding method of indicating symbol selection, location of the digits is the primary concern. Since the child does not point directly to the numbered symbols, we suggest arranging them in columns following the pattern of the Fitzgerald Key. When numbering the symbols it is advisable to skip some numbers after the last symbol in the *who* column to allow for adding symbols as the child's vocabulary grows. For example, if the last *who* symbol is number 10 the first *action* symbol might be numbered 20 instead of 11.

The digits 0 through 9 must be placed where the child can point to them.

For children with gross pointing the digit might be represented by an area covered with a colored transparent acetate. Instead of having to touch the digit the child need touch only the colored area. By the use of transparent acetate the covered area can include locations where symbols are displayed.

3. Layout for two-step coding

The matrix — the group of symbols arranged in columns and rows — should be placed where the child can easily see it. It is advisable to make this matrix on a separate card rather than directly on the poster board in order to facilitate changing its position if needed. The paired numbers and colors should be located in such positions that the observer can tell at which pair the child is looking. As the child progresses more than one matrix can be displayed. In this case the child has to indicate in some manner which matrix he is using before giving the color–number code.

It is possible to arrange symbols in a matrix following the pattern of the Fitzgerald Key. In a five by five matrix there would be five columns. Symbols might be grouped as follows:

Column 1 — five symbols for *who* words
Column 2 — five symbols for *action* words
Column 3 — five symbols for *what* words
Column 4 — five symbols for *where* words
Column 5 — five symbols for *when* words

4. Layout for scanning

In using the scanning method of communicating with symbols, the symbol user need only signal when the desired symbol is indicated. The main layout requirement is that the display be located where the symbol user can easily observe it and watch the progression of the scan. The simplest scanning is manual. The person communicating with the symbol user points to each item in the display and notes the meaning of the symbol indicated at the time the symbol user signals. Obviously, use of this system is better than being unable to communicate in any way but the fact that it makes the symbol user so dependent on the other person is a major disadvantage. Several electro-mechanical devices are now available and will be discussed later.

5. Layout for a vertical eye-pointing display

A piece of plexiglass supported in a vertical position facing the child makes a good surface on which to display symbols. A center portion is removed to facilitate face-to-face interaction between the communicators. Words of high functional value are symbolized around the perimeter (see Figure 13). This device might also be used in linear encoding by placing the digits around the perimeter (see Figure 14). Communication begins with the child looking through the cut-out section at the face of the other person, who

Figure 13. Layout on vertical plexiglass for direct selection with eye-pointing

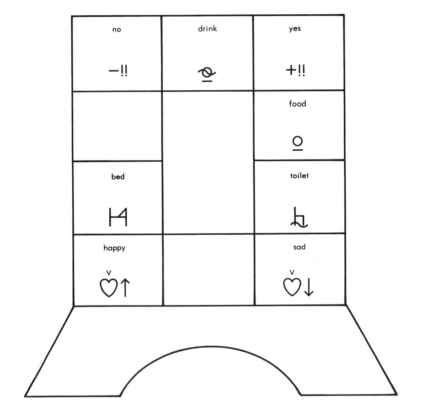

sits in front of the child with the symbol display between them. The child then directs his gaze to a number or symbol and continues looking until the other person orally identifies the symbol. The child returns his gaze to the other's face and then looks at another symbol. This procedure is continued until the message is completed. An eye-directed display for more advanced symbol users has been developed at the Ontario Crippled Children's Centre. The two-part program is designed to advance the user from System A, which displays up to 48 symbols, to System B, which displays up to 144 models (see Figure 15).

Figure 14. Layout on vertical plexiglass for linear coding using eye-pointing

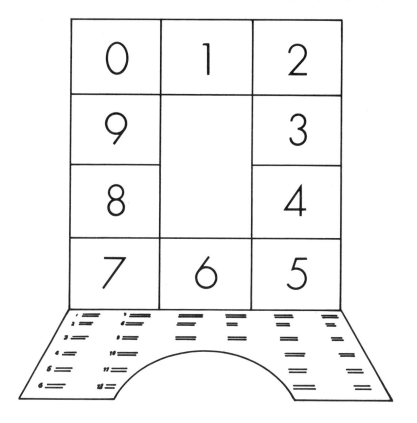

Figure 15. OCCC Eye-Directed Symbol Display

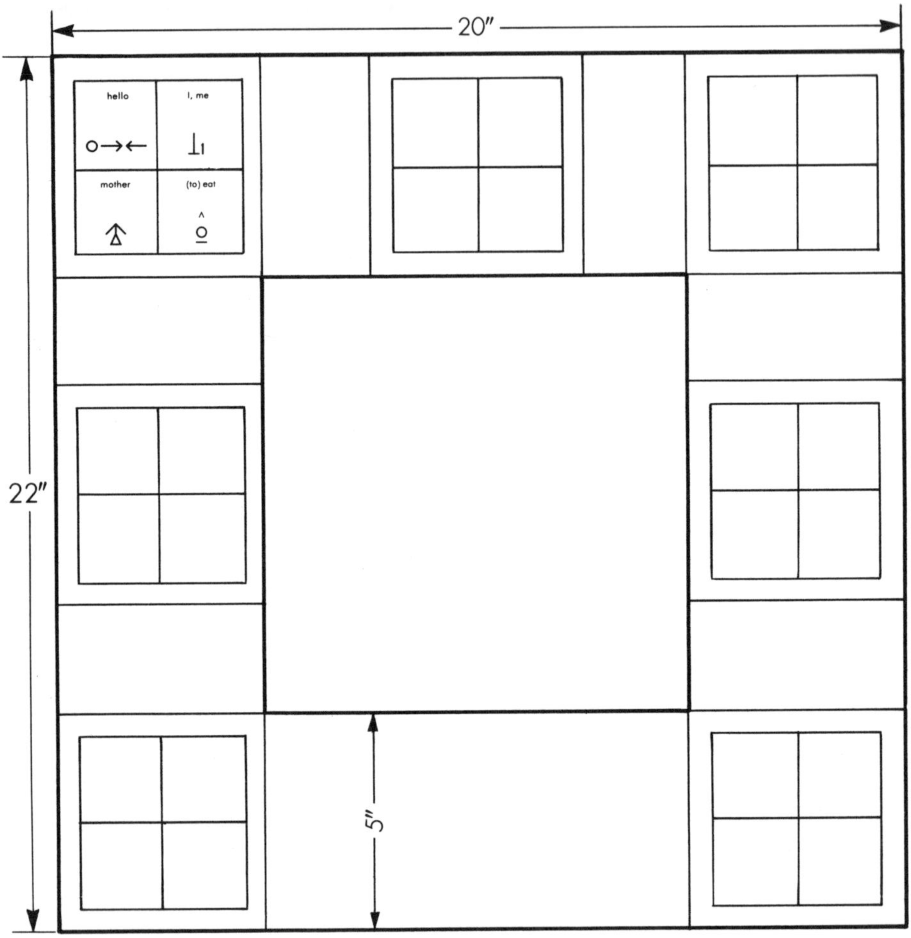

System A

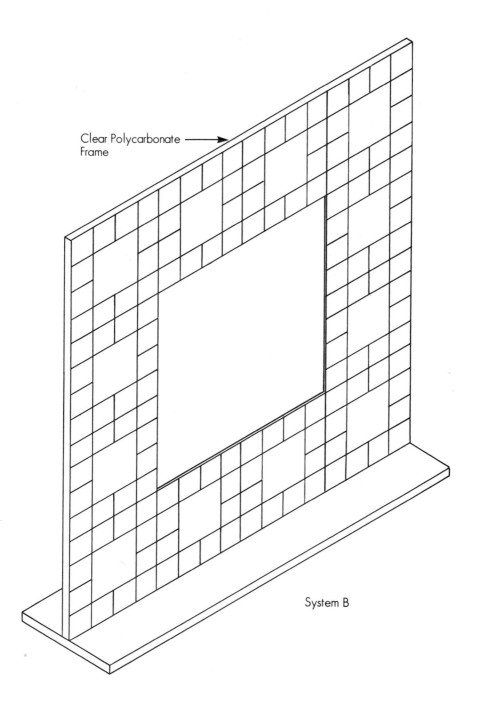

Clear Polycarbonate Frame

System B

System A. Using this system, a person can indicate with only two eye movements any symbol on the display. The display size used is 20 inches high by 20 inches wide, leaving a 5 inch frame which allows a comfortable cut-out in the middle to obtain good eye contact, as shown in Figure 15.

To introduce the system to a young child, one can use at first a simple hard cover cut to the exact size of the plastic frame and attached to the frame with tape. Partition off at each corner a quadrant and frame each corner with a different color. Divide each quadrant into four. Each symbol introduced will receive a colored frame correspondent to the position inside the quadrant, e.g. if the upper right corner is green, then every symbol positioned in this corner will have a green background. For the viewer a reversed display has to be made. All the child has to do to indicate a symbol is first establish eye contact with the viewer, then look at the quadrant where the symbol is located, have eye contact with the person, then indicate with the second look the color representing the position of the wanted symbol in the quadrant.

After the sixteen places in all four corners have been filled with symbols, additional blocks of four symbols can be added using the same system until a total of forty-eight symbols are within the display.

System B. Introducing System B with an ultimate goal of 144 symbols requires only minor adjustment, as basically the same system is used with an increased vocabulary. For each display in progression a change of position of symbols is inevitable. For a slow learner each centre of a quadrant will have a different color and each symbol within a given quadrant the correspondent color. By using Letraset over the black and white stamps a better uniform coloring can be achieved. Letraset has also a wide range of color shades, which facilitates the choice of twelve different colors. At first, the system looks overwhelmingly colorful. As soon as the child learns the system and does not rely on the color alone, he will be able to indicate by the position and the colors can be removed if desired. To obtain a more permanent display that is quite professional looking, proceed with the following instructions:

1. Take a grid for Blissymbol stamps.
2. Arrange black/white stamps in the exact order as on your display.
3. Blank out the centre of the frame with a piece of white paper. Do the same inside each quadrant.
4. Take your master to a professional photographic reproduction company and have the display enlarged to 20 inches *including* the black lines onto a clear film. (The cost will be about $4.00 to $6.00.)

5. Cut to exact size of frame and attach with clear tape.
6. As most people can read a word in reverse, no second display for the person who wants to communicate with the child is needed. A frame with such a clear plastic display can be left in an upright position on the child's lap tray as it does not obstruct his vision for driving his wheelchair.

Constructing displays for ambulatory children

Children who can walk even though they use aids such as crutches and walkers are likely to have adequate pointing skills. Their problem is that of carrying a symbol display as they move about. One solution is to construct a direct selection type display on a lightweight but durable vinyl material. A plastic place mat, for example, provides a good backing for mounting the symbols. The display is covered with clear contact paper. It may be attached to a waist band or shoulder harness with velcro or a clip or it can be hung on a walker.

To display a larger number of symbols a folder arrangement can be used. Presentation display folders available at office supply stores are useful in constructing symbol displays for some ambulatory children. The backs are sturdy and, when open, expose two large clear plastic pockets designed for displaying pictures of products. Cards on which symbols have been arranged may be inserted in the pockets thus making a symbol folder. Multi-folding units are also available. (See the *Handbook of Blissymbolics*, pp.235–286 for other suggestions.)

Electro-mechanical displays

For some non-speaking individuals, electro-mechanical communication aids have numerous advantages. It would be a serious mistake, however, to postpone communication training until a suitable electro-mechanical aid became available. When initiating a symbol program with young children the simple ''home-made'' communication displays are more appropriate. The communication skills and the knowledge of Blissymbols acquired with the simple displays will provide a sound basis for communication when the child ''graduates'' to a sophisticated electro-mechanical aid.

It would be inappropriate to discuss here all the electro-mechanical communication aids that have been described in various publications or at professional meetings. The state of the art is changing rapidly. Cumbersome, expensive electro-mechanical devices are becoming smaller and less expensive. The *Trace Research and Development Center for the Severely Communicatively Handicapped* (314 Waisman Center, 1500 Highland Avenue, Madison, Wisconsin 53706) has published a comprehensive annotated list of communication aids and as a professional service, regularly updates this list. Many of the aids described exist only as prototypes and it may be some time before they become commercially available. Following are a few examples of commercially available devices that may be used for accessing Blissymbols.

1. Bliss Symbol Scanners

Bliss Symbol scanners are available from the Prentke-Romich Company (R.D. 2, Shreve, Ohio 44676), which is licensed by the Blissymbolics Communication Institute to provide communication aids using Blissymbols. Symbols and their meanings are displayed in rows and columns. Each symbol location has a small lamp in the corner. By operating a simple control switch the symbol user can scan, at an adjustable rate, the symbol locations. When the desired location is reached the symbol user again operates the switch causing the lamp at that location to flash on and off. A memory unit is available allowing the symbol user to store up to 64 symbols which can later be displayed in sequence; hence an observer need not be present while the symbol message is being assembled. Other symbols may be used by drawing them on a white coated plastic display mask which fits over the surface of the scanner.

2. Zygo Communications Systems

This system is available from Everest and Jennings, Inc. (1803 Pontious Avenue, Los Angeles, California 90025). The scanning unit was not designed specifically for Blissymbols but symbols may be drawn on the display area. A variety of mechanisms which may be operated by touch, breathing, biting, etc. is available for interrupting the scanning sequence to indicate the desired symbol. To facilitate training it is possible to reduce the number of display areas used and increase them as symbol learning progresses.

3. Autocom

The autocom is available from Telesensory Systems, Inc. (3408 Hillview Avenue, P.O. Box 10099, Palo Alto, California 94304). A direct selection device developed at the Trace Center, it has become a complex unit with many outputs, such as a message viewer, a printer, a TV display and a device for sending messages over the phone to persons who have a print-out device. The user holds a small magnet over the symbol chosen and an electronic circuit causes that letter, word or symbol to be shown in the output device. The outputs are in traditional orthography — letters, words and conventional symbols — as are the displays. It would be possible to substitute Blissymbols on the surface display. Through appropriate programming pointing to a Blissymbol would cause the word it symbolizes to appear in the output.

In cooperation with the BCI the Trace Center is developing a Blissymbol Printer.

4. HandiVoice

HandiVoice is available from HC Electronics, Inc. (250 Camino Alto, Mill Valley, California 94941). This direct-selection device, which is small enough to hold in the hand, produces synthesized speech. In one model, 473 sounds, words and phrases are accessed through a touch-sensitive, pre-programmed keyboard. The display is in traditional orthography but it would be possible to substitute appropriate Blissymbols for the pre-programmed words. It is not possible to change the words nor to rearrange them; hence, this aid has only limited usefulness in the Blissymbol program.

5. Form-a-Phrase

This device is available from SciTronics, Inc. (523 So. Clewell Street, P.O. Box 5344, Bethlehem, PA 18015). Words, phrases or sentences of up to five words, which have been pre-recorded in a natural voice on an eight track cartridge, may be accessed either by direct selection or a scanning technique. For the direct selection method, the vocabulary is printed in a changeable laminated card which fastens to the "wordboard." The wordboard can also serve as a tray. Selections from the display are made by moving a hand-held magnet over the desired item, causing the unit to reproduce the pre-recorded utterance. Blissymbols representing the pre-recorded material may be drawn on a laminated card to replace the printed display. A standard set of utterances is available and it is possible to have a customized set prepared using an adult's or a child's voice.

It is also possible to operate the unit in a scanning mode, using a variety of control switches.

Considerations in selecting an electro-mechanical aid

Before recommending or obtaining an electro-mechanical communication device for an orally-handicapped individual the following factors should be considered.

1. Is the child's level of cognitive functioning adequate for learning to use the communication aid?

Severely retarded children with low level language development are not likely to derive much benefit from a communication aid. It is possible that the complexities of operating the aid might interfere with language learning. For some, use of an aid might stimulate language acquisition but arrangements should be made to try one before purchase.

2. How is the unit controlled?

Unless the handicapped person can operate the control switches the aid will be useless. Study the switches available with the unit and if possible have the handicapped person experiment with them. It might be possible for an electronic technician to construct a suitable switch from available designs (see *Handbook of Blissymbolics*, pp.287–309) but, again, have the child try the switch before purchasing the communication aid.

3. What is the nature of the display seen by the handicapped person?

The number and size of individual units arranged on the display surface is important. Some children would be confused by having too many symbols displayed, whereas an advanced symbol user would get little benefit from an aid that allowed access to only a few symbols. Consider also if Blissymbols can be used in the display and if the displays can be changed as the child's communication abilities and needs change.

4. What is the nature of the output?

The output of some aids is a light which flashes or remains on to indicate the user's choice. Some aids give a vocalized output (synthetic or natural speech) and others give a graphic print out. Determine if the output can be stored to be recalled and displayed later or if the observer must be present to assemble the message as it is being constructed.

5. How will the aid be used?

Think about with whom and where the child is likely to communicate and consider the problems of having the communication aid available at those times. Most aids are described as "portable" but the handicapped persons may have to rely on someone else to move them about.

6. What is the initial cost and what services are available for maintenance and repair?

The potential market for electro-mechanical communication devices is small, so high volume production is not feasible. This factor tends to keep costs high, especially during the early period of production and marketing. For some handicapped persons even a high initial cost is warranted because of the effect the aid will have on their lives. Other persons will get so little benefit from an aid that it is logical to weigh cost versus benefit.

Appendix A

Purposes and services of the Blissymbolics Communication Institute

The Blissymbolics Communication Institute is a non-profit corporation chartered under the laws of the Province of Ontario, Canada. To this corporation C. K. Bliss, who holds registered copyrights to Blissymbolics, has assigned the right to use the symbols and symbol system by way of an exclusive, world-wide and perpetual license to use, publish, teach and disseminate Blissymbolics.

The Blissymbolics Communication Institute lists the following as its purposes:

1. to develop and maintain standards for Blissymbols;
2. to develop and maintain standards of training in Blissymbolics;
3. to disseminate information regarding Blissymbolics;
4. to develop and distribute symbol displays and instructional aids and materials;
5. to collect information regarding the use of Blissymbolics as a communication system for non-speaking persons;
6. to collect information regarding other applications of Blissymbolics;
7. to promote exchange of information through serving as a liaison between symbol users and their families and instructors, researchers, educational institutions, government and social agencies, and producers of materials and technical aids.

An important activity of BCI is the training of professional and para-professional workers. Approved training sessions offer basic instruction in the Blissymbolics system and its application and lead to certification. These are held at the BCI in Toronto, Ontario, and at Resource Centres which are sub-licensed by BCI as local Blissymbolics Training and Information centers. By special arrangements, workshops may be conducted in other settings. *Special interest workshops* focus on the application of symbols with specific populations, for example, pre-school children, retarded persons, adult aphasics, or on special topics such as the relation between Blissymbols and reading. *In-service training* programs are designed to give an overview of the Bliss system and its application and do not lead to certification for the participants. *Internship training* is an intensive program of study and practice offered in Toronto.

Associate Membership in the Blissymbolics Communication Institute is available, for an annual fee, to any person or organization interested in supporting the BCI in the development of Blissymbolics. A new symbol user's membership is now available at a greatly reduced rate. It is made possible through a subsidy from the other memberships. Privileges and duties of Associate Members include:

1. to promote the objectives of the Blissymbolics Communication Institute throughout the world in using, or teaching or assisting in the development of symbol communication;
2. to advise the Blissymbolics Communication Institute individually or in meetings called for the purpose as to symbol usage and development;
3. to be informed by the Blissymbolics Communication Institute of current usage and events concerning symbol development;
4. to assist those whose own language skills are inadequate by providing a workable symbol communication system.

Services and materials

1. Periodical publications

Dissemination of information is an important BCI service. *The Bulletin*, published three times a year, carries information, discusses trends in the use of Blissymbolics and reports BCI activities. It is distributed without charge to Associate Members. As new publications are available, new electro-mechanical systems are constructed or new teaching materials are developed they will be announced in *The Bulletin. The Newsletter*, also published three times a year, carries articles and news items about Blissymbolics which are written by professional and lay people to share ideas and experiences growing out of their involvement in symbol communication. It is distributed without charge to Associate Members.

2. Books

Blissymbols for Use, compiled and edited by Barbara Hehner. This book contains over 1400 Blissymbols, arranged in two categories: *Finding*

Symbols (arranged by the structure of the symbols) and *Finding Meanings* (symbols related in meaning are grouped together). There is also an *Index* of all English equivalents for symbols used in the book, a number of notes explaining key points in symbol grammar, and a full explanation of the symbol alphabet now used to arrange Blissymbol stamps and flashcards.

Handbook of Blissymbolics: This volume was written for instructors, symbol users, parents and administrators. The 650 pages are assembled in loose-leaf form to facilitate updating in response to future developments in Blissymbol programs. Part I of the Handbook contains the following major sections: The Blissymbol System, Physical Functional Considerations, Application of the System, and Appendices that describe interfaces, teaching aids and materials, programming aids, commercially available aids and other sources of information, extension of the program into the community, response to common misconceptions regarding Blissymbolics as a communication medium for non-speaking physically handicapped persons, and eye pointing. Part II is a report of "A Formative Evaluation Study" which was initiated in 1974 to collect information from instructors in a variety of settings regarding the effectiveness of the symbol system, based on their records of symbol performance and their experience in providing instruction. A condensed paperback edition of this book is planned.

Symbol Secrets by Shirley McNaughton. An illustrated children's book (to be enjoyed by all ages), which presents the "secrets" of the first Blissymbol users. Through this sharing, the author hopes to encourage the enjoyment and acceptance of Blissymbol communication through a greater understanding of its users.

3. Audio-visual materials

Video tapes, audio tapes (cassettes), films and slides are available at a small service charge, for use in public relations programs and in-service training. As new materials become available they will be described in *The Bulletin*. Of particular interest are the following:

Video tapes:

Parent Involvement. Family experiences with a symbol user and effect on family and friends. (30 minutes)

Individual Children. Three children using symbols, one at elementary level, one at fluent level and one severely involved child. (20 minutes)

Joseph Kaeble School. Discussion by principal and teacher of problems encountered in integrating a symbol user into a regular classroom. (50 minutes)

Sensory City. General outline and teacher discussion of symbol program in three OCCC classrooms: kindergarten, severely involved, and advanced. Presents classroom scenes. (40 minutes)

Films:

Mr. Symbol Man. 16mm color study of Charles K. Bliss' work, co-produced by the National Film Board of Canada and Film Australia (1974).

MacKay Centre, Montreal. 16mm color film which includes a brief interview with Shirley McNaughton, short sequence of Charles Bliss from *Mr. Symbol Man*, scenes of a child using symbols at school and at home, interview with child's teacher and parents.

Slides:

Say it with Symbols is a teaching series designed by the BCI and the National Film Board of Canada. The 750 slides and accompanying teaching manual are designed to present the meaning and use of approximately 250 symbols.

Symbol stamps:

Approximately 1400 symbols are available in booklet form, printed on water repellent, non-glare material backed with permanent adhesive. The two sizes, $7/8$ inch square or $9/16$ inch square are available in color coding or in black and white, and in French or English, with other languages planned for the future. Individual stamps may be removed from the sheet.

Flash cards:

A vocabulary of 250 symbols (black on white or color-coded) is printed on a $2^5/8$ inch square. This square covers an area of 3 x 3 inches on the larger stamp grid. The cards are suitable for drills and games or as large symbols for an introductory display. They are available in French or English.

Templates:

The following templates for drawing symbols are available:

large imperial — large square is 1 inch

large metric — large square is 20 mm (approximately $3/4$ inch)

small metric — large square is 10 mm (approximately $1/2$ inch)

Appendix B

Enlarging Blissymbols

Several sizes of ready-drawn symbols are available. Two sizes of stamps have been printed — a $9/16$ inch square and a $7/8$ inch square. (These are stamp sizes — the symbols are smaller.) On the 3 x 3 inch square flash cards the symbols are drawn to the scale of a $2^5/8$ inch square. Three templates are available. On the large imperial template, symbols are scaled to a 1 inch square, on the large metric template, symbols are scaled to a 20 mm square (approximately $3/4$ inch), and on the small metric template, symbols are scaled to a 10 mm square (approximately $1/2$ inch).

It is sometimes necessary to produce larger symbols for bulletin boards, labels, signs or other uses. Correctly proportioned symbols can be drawn to any size using either of the two methods described below.

Dividing a square

Decide how large you want the *heart* symbol to be. This will establish the dimensions of the square which is to be the frame of reference for drawing the enlarged symbols. Follow these steps to develop a guide for drawing the symbols.

1. Draw in pencil a square to the desired dimensions.
2. Divide each side into quarters.
3. Divide the large square into four smaller squares.
4. Draw symbol and erase guidelines. Remember that larger symbols require thicker lines.

Projecting transparencies

For this procedure you will need a projector for 2 x 2 inch slides and access to equipment for making transparencies of the type used with an overhead projector. Follow these steps:

Figure 16. Enlarging Symbols

1. Square may be of
   any size.

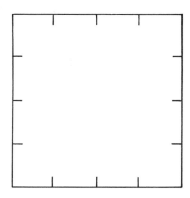

2. Divide sides
   into quarters.

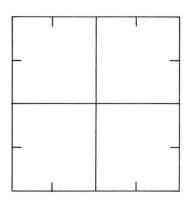

3. Divide larger
   square into
   four squares.

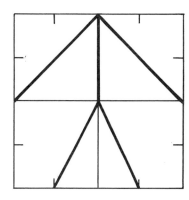

4. Draw symbol
   and erase guidelines.

1. Line a sheet of white 8½ x 11 inch paper to divide it into rectangles 40 mm long x 35 mm wide. This size will fit into a 2 x 2 inch slide holder (see Figure 17).
2. Remove from a set of symbol stamps those symbols you want to enlarge.
3. Stick each symbol on the white paper centered in one of the rectangles.
4. Make a transparency of the sheet with mounted symbols.
5. Cut the transparencies into 40 x 35 mm rectangles.

6. Mount in 2 x 2 inch slide holders. These are available in photo-
   graphy stores.
7. Tape the display material (e.g., poster board) to a wall and project
   the symbol on it as if it were a screen.
8. Vary the distance between projector and display material until
   image is of desired size.
9. Trace image.

Figure 17. Projecting Transparencies

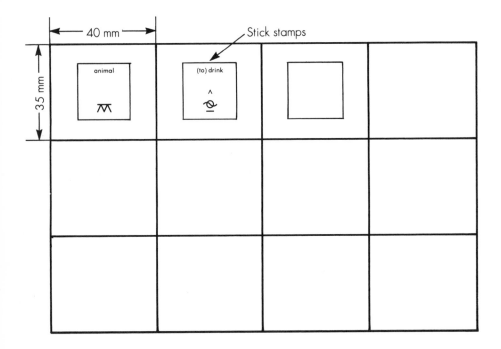

Bibliography

Bliss, C. K., *Semantography*, Sydney, Australia: Semantography Publications, 1965.

Bliss, C. K., *The Book to the Film 'Mr. Symbol Man,'* Sydney, Australia: Semantography Publications, 1975.

Connor, F. P., Williamson, G. G., and Siepp, S. M., *Program Guide for Infants and Toddlers with Neuromotor and other Developmental Disabilities*, New York: Teachers College Press, 1978.

Dyan, M., Harper, B., Molloy, J. S., and Witt, B. T., *Communication for the Severely and Profoundly Handicapped*, Denver, Co: Love Publishing Company, 1977.

Fitzgerald, E., *Straight Language for the Deaf: A System of Instruction for Deaf Children*, Austin, Texas: Steck and Co., 1937.

Harris-Vanderheiden, D., Brown, W. P., Reinen, S., MacKenzie, P., and Scheibel, C., "Symbol Communication for the Mentally Retarded," *Mental Retardation*, Vol. 13, No. 1 (February, 1975).

Hehner, B. (ed.), *Blissymbols for Use,* Toronto, Canada: Blissymbolics Communication Institute, 1980.

Helfman, E. S., *Signs and Symbols around the World*, New York: Lothrop, Lee and Shepard, 1967.

Kent, L. R., *Language Acquisition Program for the Severely Retarded*, Champaign, Ill.: Research Press, 1974.

Lee, L. L., Koenigsknecht, R. A., and Mulhern, S., *Interactive Language Development Teaching*, Evanston, Ill.: Northwestern University Press, 1975.

McDonald, E. T., and Schultz, A. R., "Communication Boards for Cerebral Palsied Children," *Journal of Speech and Hearing Disorders*, 38, (February, 1973), 73–88.

Moskowitz, B. A., "The Acquisition of Language," *Scientific American*, November 1978, 92–108.

Pugh, B. L., *Steps in Language Development for the Deaf Illustrated in The Fitzgerald Key*, Washington, D.C.: Volta Bureau, 1965.

Pulaski, M. A. S., *Understanding Piaget*, New York: Harper and Row, 1971.

Schiefelbusch, R. L. (ed.), *Bases of Language Intervention*, Baltimore: University Park Press, 1978.

Silverman, H., McNaughton, S., and Kates, B., *Handbook of Blissymbolics*, Toronto, Canada: Blissymbolics Communication Institute, 1978.

Vanderheiden, G. C. and Grilley, K., *Non-Vocal Communication Techniques and Aids for the Severely Physically Handicapped*, Baltimore: University Park Press, 1975.

Vicker, B. (ed.) *Nonoral Communication System Project 1964/73*, Iowa City, Iowa: Campus Stores, University of Iowa, 1974.

Index